Cocoas, Cappuccinos, Coffees & Teas

Recipes to make your own gifts

Use these recipes to delight your friends and family. Each recipe includes gift tags for your convenience — just cut them out and personalize!

To decorate jars, cut fabric in 9" diameter circles. Screw down the jar ring to hold fabric in place or hold fabric with a ribbon, raffia, twine, yarn, lace or string (first secure the fabric with a rubber band before tying). Punch a hole into the corner of the tag and use the ribbon, raffia, twine, yarn, lace or string to attach the tag to the jar.

These gifts should keep for up to six months.

Printed in China

Distributed By:

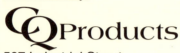

507 Industrial Street
Waverly, IA 50677

ISBN 1-56383-134-1

Mocha Fireside Coffee Mix

1 2/3 C. powdered coffee creamer
1 1/3 C. instant hot cocoa mix
2/3 C. instant coffee granules
2/3 C. powdered chocolate flavored drink mix
2 T. plus 2 tsp. sugar
1 1/4 tsp. plus 1/8 tsp. ground cinnamon
1/4 tsp. plus 1/8 tsp. ground nutmeg

In a large bowl, combine the above ingredients and stir until the mixture is well blended. Place mix in a wide-mouth 1-quart canning jar.

Attach a gift tag with the directions on how to prepare the coffee.

Mocha Fireside Coffee

To make one serving:
1 T. Mocha Fireside Coffee Mix
6 oz. (3/4 C.) boiling water
Whipped cream and shaved
chocolate, optional

Place the Mocha Fireside Coffee Mix in a mug. Pour boiling water over the mixture. Stir until the mix is completely dissolved. If desired, garnish with whipped cream and shaved chocolate.

Mocha Fireside Coffee

To make one serving:
1 T. Mocha Fireside Coffee Mix
6 oz. (3/4 C.) boiling water

Whipped cream and shaved
chocolate, optional

Place the Mocha Fireside Coffee Mix in a mug. Pour boiling water over the mixture. Stir until the mix is completely dissolved. If desired, garnish with whipped cream and shaved chocolate.

Mocha Fireside Coffee

To make one serving:
1 T. Mocha Fireside Coffee Mix
6 oz. (3/4 C.) boiling water

Whipped cream and shaved
chocolate, optional

Place the Mocha Fireside Coffee Mix in a mug. Pour boiling water over the mixture. Stir until the mix is completely dissolved. If desired, garnish with whipped cream and shaved chocolate.

Mocha Fireside Coffee

To make one serving:
1 T. Mocha Fireside Coffee Mix
6 oz. (3/4 C.) boiling water

Whipped cream and shaved
chocolate, optional

Place the Mocha Fireside Coffee Mix in a mug. Pour boiling water over the mixture. Stir until the mix is completely dissolved. If desired, garnish with whipped cream and shaved chocolate.

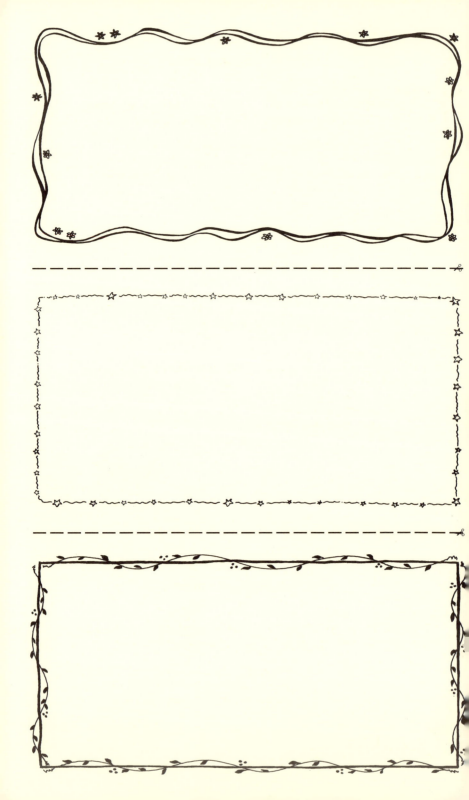

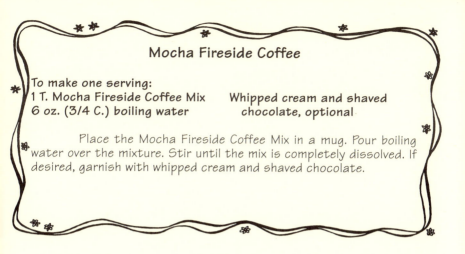

Mocha Fireside Coffee

To make one serving:
1 T. Mocha Fireside Coffee Mix   Whipped cream and shaved
6 oz. (3/4 C.) boiling water   chocolate, optional

    Place the Mocha Fireside Coffee Mix in a mug. Pour boiling water over the mixture. Stir until the mix is completely dissolved. If desired, garnish with whipped cream and shaved chocolate.

Mocha Fireside Coffee

To make one serving:
1 T. Mocha Fireside Coffee Mix   Whipped cream and shaved
6 oz. (3/4 C.) boiling water   chocolate, optional

    Place the Mocha Fireside Coffee Mix in a mug. Pour boiling water over the mixture. Stir until the mix is completely dissolved. If desired, garnish with whipped cream and shaved chocolate.

Mocha Fireside Coffee

To make one serving:
1 T. Mocha Fireside Coffee Mix   Whipped cream and shaved
6 oz. (3/4 C.) boiling water   chocolate, optional

    Place the Mocha Fireside Coffee Mix in a mug. Pour boiling water over the mixture. Stir until the mix is completely dissolved. If desired, garnish with whipped cream and shaved chocolate.

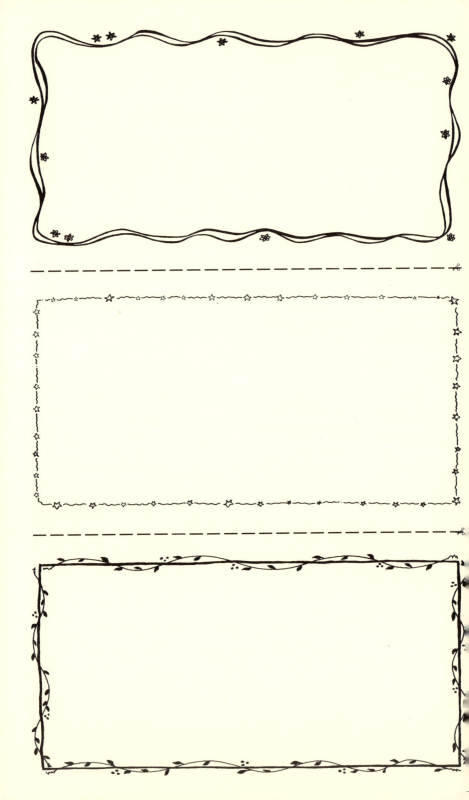

French Vanilla Cappuccino Mix

1 1/3 C. sugar
1 1/3 C. French Vanilla flavored
   powdered coffee creamer
2/3 C. powdered instant dry milk
2/3 C. instant coffee granules

In a large bowl, combine the above ingredients and stir until the mixture is well blended. Place mix in a wide-mouth 1-quart canning jar.

Attach a gift tag with the directions on how to prepare the cappuccino.

❀ *A half-yard of fabric should make eight wide-mouth jar covers.* ❀

French Vanilla Cappuccino

To make one serving:
4 tsp. French Vanilla Cappuccino
** Mix**
8 oz. (1 C.) boiling water

Place the French Vanilla Cappuccino Mix in a mug. Pour boiling water over the mixture. Stir until the mix is completely dissolved.

French Vanilla Cappuccino

To make one serving:
4 tsp. French Vanilla
Cappuccino Mix

8 oz. (1 C.) boiling water

Place the French Vanilla Cappuccino Mix in a mug. Pour boiling water over the mixture. Stir until the mix is completely dissolved.

French Vanilla Cappuccino

To make one serving:
4 tsp. French Vanilla
Cappuccino Mix

8 oz. (1 C.) boiling water

Place the French Vanilla Cappuccino Mix in a mug. Pour boiling water over the mixture. Stir until the mix is completely dissolved.

French Vanilla Cappuccino

To make one serving:
4 tsp. French Vanilla
Cappuccino Mix

8 oz. (1 C.) boiling water

Place the French Vanilla Cappuccino Mix in a mug. Pour boiling water over the mixture. Stir until the mix is completely dissolved.

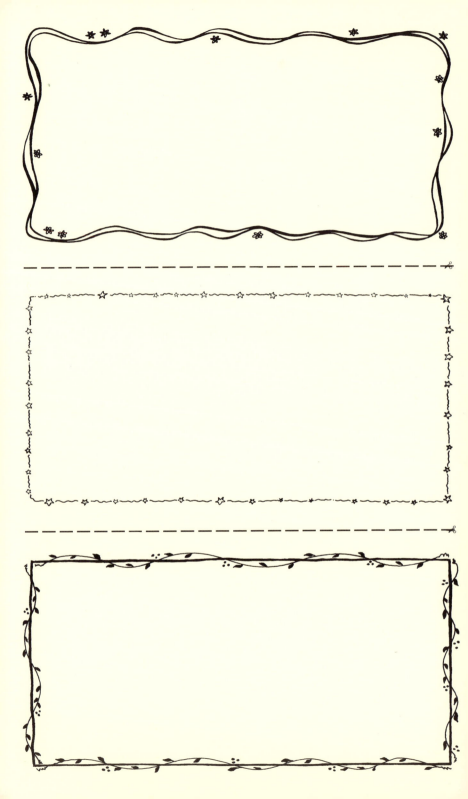

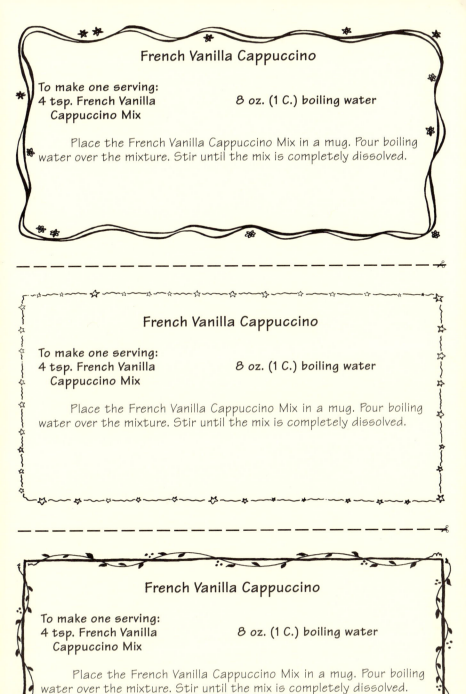

French Vanilla Cappuccino

To make one serving:
4 tsp. French Vanilla
 Cappuccino Mix

8 oz. (1 C.) boiling water

   Place the French Vanilla Cappuccino Mix in a mug. Pour boiling water over the mixture. Stir until the mix is completely dissolved.

French Vanilla Cappuccino

To make one serving:
4 tsp. French Vanilla
 Cappuccino Mix

8 oz. (1 C.) boiling water

   Place the French Vanilla Cappuccino Mix in a mug. Pour boiling water over the mixture. Stir until the mix is completely dissolved.

French Vanilla Cappuccino

To make one serving:
4 tsp. French Vanilla
 Cappuccino Mix

8 oz. (1 C.) boiling water

   Place the French Vanilla Cappuccino Mix in a mug. Pour boiling water over the mixture. Stir until the mix is completely dissolved.

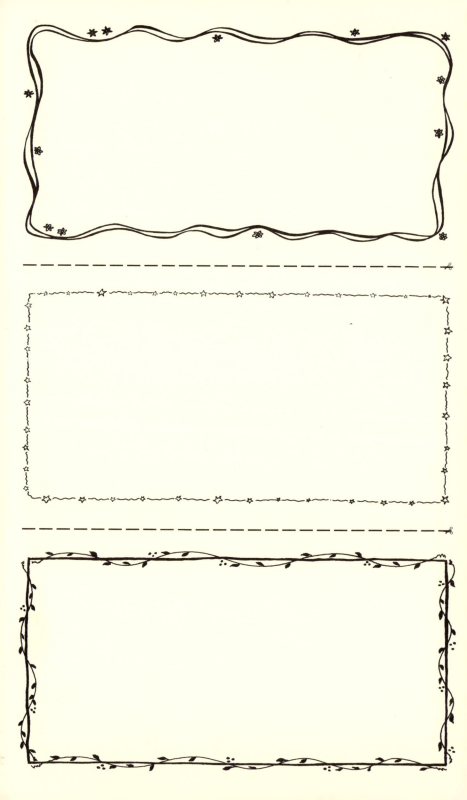

Heartwarming Tea Mix

1 jar (15 oz.) powdered orange
   flavored drink mix
1 C. sugar
1 C. unsweetened instant tea
1/2 C. presweetened lemonade
   mix
1 tsp. imitation pineapple
   extract
1 tsp. imitation coconut extract

In a blender or food processor, combine the above ingredients until the mixture is well blended. Place mix in a wide-mouth 1-quart canning jar.

Attach a gift tag with the directions on how to prepare the tea.

❀ *For holiday gifts, tie a candy cane or two to the outside of the jar to help with the stirring.* ❀

Heartwarming Tea

To make one serving:
1 rounded T. Heartwarming Tea Mix
6 oz. (3/4 C.) boiling water

Place the Heartwarming Tea Mix in a mug. Pour boiling water over the mixture. Stir until the mix is completely dissolved.

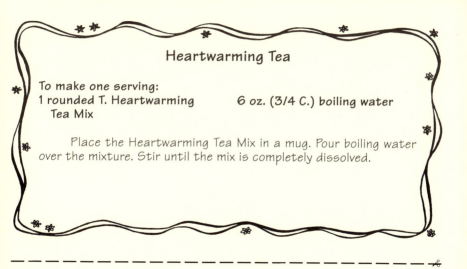

Heartwarming Tea

To make one serving:
1 rounded T. Heartwarming   6 oz. (3/4 C.) boiling water
   Tea Mix

Place the Heartwarming Tea Mix in a mug. Pour boiling water over the mixture. Stir until the mix is completely dissolved.

Heartwarming Tea

To make one serving:
1 rounded T. Heartwarming   6 oz. (3/4 C.) boiling water
   Tea Mix

Place the Heartwarming Tea Mix in a mug. Pour boiling water over the mixture. Stir until the mix is completely dissolved.

Heartwarming Tea

To make one serving:
1 rounded T. Heartwarming   6 oz. (3/4 C.) boiling water
   Tea Mix

Place the Heartwarming Tea Mix in a mug. Pour boiling water over the mixture. Stir until the mix is completely dissolved.

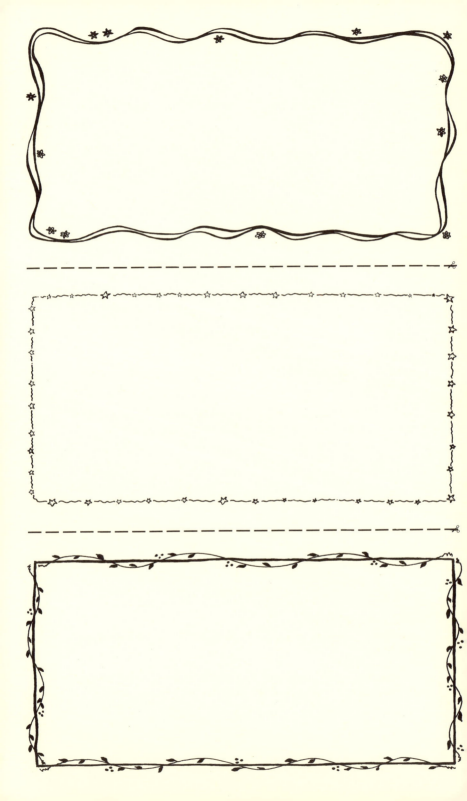

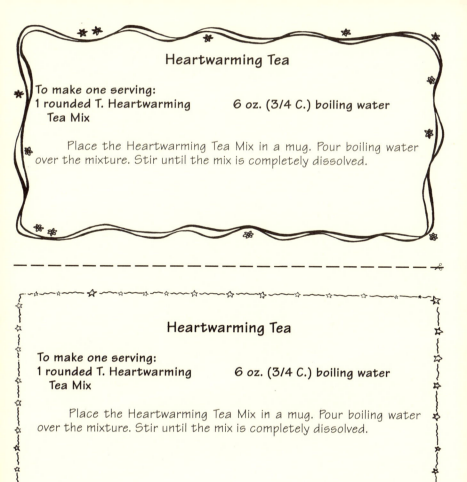

Heartwarming Tea

To make one serving:
1 rounded T. Heartwarming   6 oz. (3/4 C.) boiling water
   Tea Mix

    Place the Heartwarming Tea Mix in a mug. Pour boiling water over the mixture. Stir until the mix is completely dissolved.

Heartwarming Tea

To make one serving:
1 rounded T. Heartwarming   6 oz. (3/4 C.) boiling water
   Tea Mix

    Place the Heartwarming Tea Mix in a mug. Pour boiling water over the mixture. Stir until the mix is completely dissolved.

Heartwarming Tea

To make one serving:
1 rounded T. Heartwarming   6 oz. (3/4 C.) boiling water
   Tea Mix

    Place the Heartwarming Tea Mix in a mug. Pour boiling water over the mixture. Stir until the mix is completely dissolved.

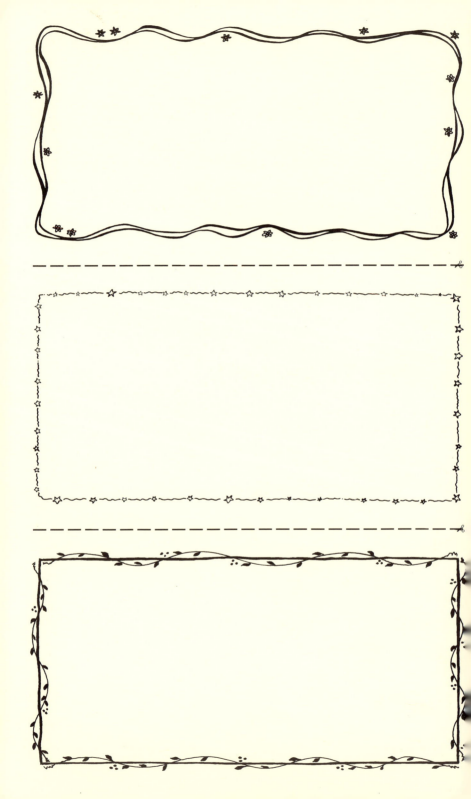

Viennese Coffee Mix

1 1/3 C. instant coffee granules
1 1/3 C. sugar
1 1/2 C. powdered coffee creamer
1 tsp. ground cinnamon
2 dashes ground allspice
2 dashes ground cloves
2 dashes ground nutmeg

In a large bowl, combine the above ingredients and stir until the mixture is well blended. Place mix in a wide-mouth 1-quart canning jar.

Attach a gift tag with the directions on how to prepare the coffee.

Viennese Coffee

To make one serving:
4 heaping tsp. Viennese
**   Coffee Mix**
8 oz. (1 C.) boiling water

Place the Viennese Coffee Mix in a mug. Pour boiling water over the mixture. Stir until the mix is completely dissolved.

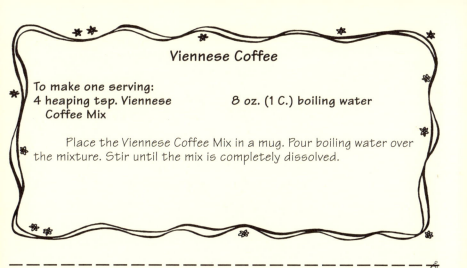

Viennese Coffee

To make one serving:

4 heaping tsp. Viennese
   Coffee Mix

8 oz. (1 C.) boiling water

   Place the Viennese Coffee Mix in a mug. Pour boiling water over
the mixture. Stir until the mix is completely dissolved.

Viennese Coffee

To make one serving:

4 heaping tsp. Viennese
   Coffee Mix

8 oz. (1 C.) boiling water

   Place the Viennese Coffee Mix in a mug. Pour boiling water
over the mixture. Stir until the mix is completely dissolved.

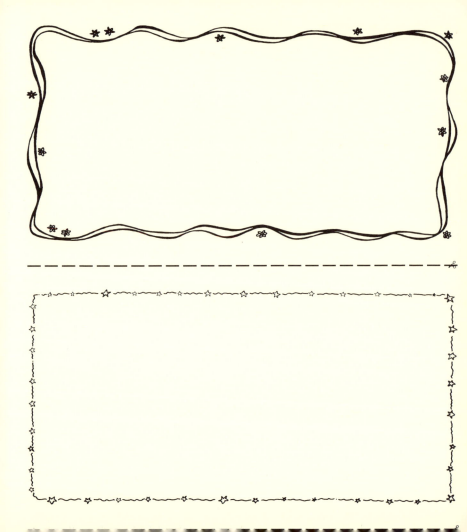

Viennese Coffee

To make one serving:
4 heaping tsp. Viennese   8 oz. (1 C.) boiling water
   Coffee Mix

   Place the Viennese Coffee Mix in a mug. Pour boiling water over
the mixture. Stir until the mix is completely dissolved.

Viennese Coffee

To make one serving:
4 heaping tsp. Viennese   8 oz. (1 C.) boiling water
   Coffee Mix

   Place the Viennese Coffee Mix in a mug. Pour boiling water
over the mixture. Stir until the mix is completely dissolved.

Viennese Coffee

To make one serving:
4 heaping tsp. Viennese   8 oz. (1 C.) boiling water
   Coffee Mix

   Place the Viennese Coffee Mix in a mug. Pour boiling water over
the mixture. Stir until the mix is completely dissolved.

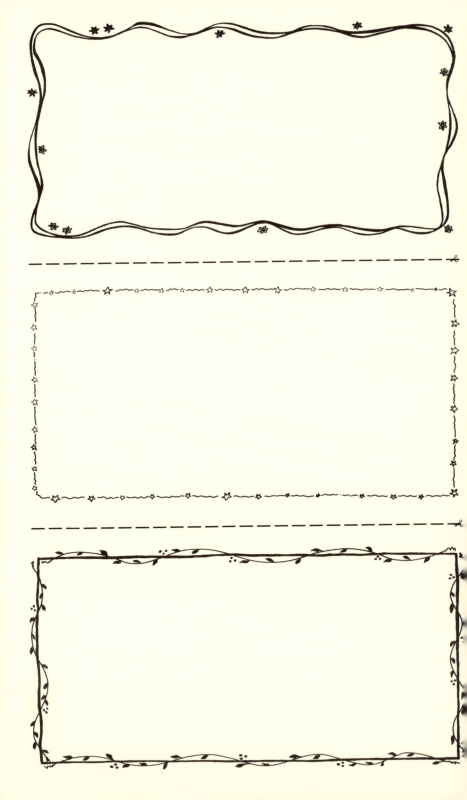

Cinnamon Hot Chocolate Mix

1 3/4 C. powdered instant dry
   milk
1 C. powdered sugar
1/2 C. powdered coffee creamer
1/2 C. unsweetened cocoa
1/2 tsp. ground cinnamon
1 C. miniature marshmallows

In a large bowl, combine the above ingredients and stir until the mixture is well blended. Place mix in a wide-mouth 1-quart canning jar.

Attach a gift tag with the directions on how to prepare the hot chocolate.

❀ For a special touch, attach chocolate covered plastic spoons to the jars. To make, dip spoons in the melted chocolate of your choice, set on wax paper, refrigerate for 30 minutes or until set, wrap individually with plastic wrap and tie off with a ribbon. ❀

Cinnamon Hot Chocolate

To make one serving:
3 T. Cinnamon Hot Chocolate
**   Mix**
6 oz. (3/4 C.) hot milk
Marshmallows, optional

Place the Cinnamon Hot Chocolate Mix in a mug. Pour the hot milk over the mixture. Stir until the mix is completely dissolved. If desired, garnish with additional marshmallows.

Cinnamon Hot Chocolate

To make one serving:
3 T. Cinnamon Hot Chocolate   Marshmallows, optional
   Mix
6 oz. (3/4 C.) hot milk

   Place the Cinnamon Hot Chocolate Mix in a mug. Pour the hot milk over the mixture. Stir until the mix is completely dissolved. If desired, garnish with additional marshmallows.

Cinnamon Hot Chocolate

To make one serving:
3 T. Cinnamon Hot Chocolate   Marshmallows, optional
   Mix
6 oz. (3/4 C.) hot milk

   Place the Cinnamon Hot Chocolate Mix in a mug. Pour the hot milk over the mixture. Stir until the mix is completely dissolved. If desired, garnish with additional marshmallows.

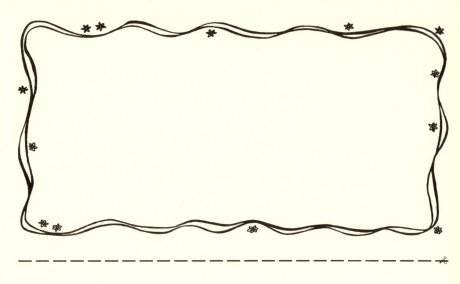

Cinnamon Hot Chocolate

To make one serving:

3 T. Cinnamon Hot Chocolate   Marshmallows, optional
   Mix
6 oz. (3/4 C.) hot milk

   Place the Cinnamon Hot Chocolate Mix in a mug. Pour the hot milk over the mixture. Stir until the mix is completely dissolved. If desired, garnish with additional marshmallows.

Cinnamon Hot Chocolate

To make one serving:

3 T. Cinnamon Hot Chocolate   Marshmallows, optional
   Mix
6 oz. (3/4 C.) hot milk

   Place the Cinnamon Hot Chocolate Mix in a mug. Pour the hot milk over the mixture. Stir until the mix is completely dissolved. If desired, garnish with additional marshmallows.

Cinnamon Hot Chocolate

To make one serving:

3 T. Cinnamon Hot Chocolate   Marshmallows, optional
   Mix
6 oz. (3/4 C.) hot milk

   Place the Cinnamon Hot Chocolate Mix in a mug. Pour the hot milk over the mixture. Stir until the mix is completely dissolved. If desired, garnish with additional marshmallows.

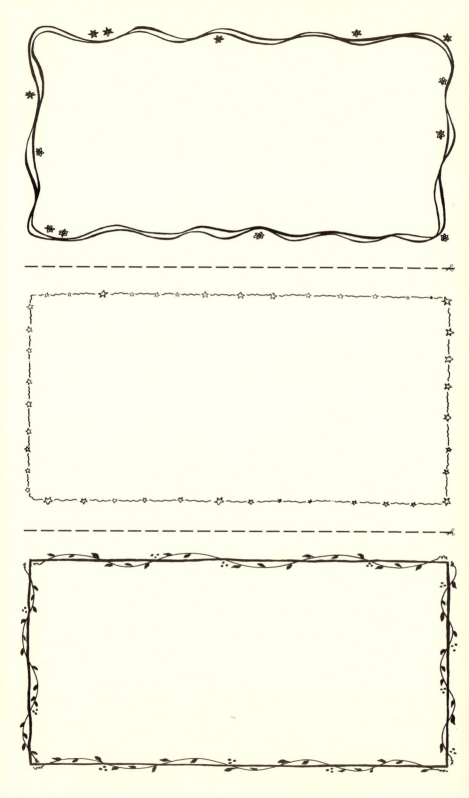

Hot Chocolate Mix

3 1/2 C. powdered instant dry
   milk
2 C. sifted powdered sugar
1 C. powdered coffee creamer
1/2 C. unsweetened cocoa
Dash salt

In a large bowl, combine the above ingredients and stir until the mixture is well blended. Place mix in a wide-mouth 1-quart canning jar.

Attach a gift tag with the directions on how to prepare the hot chocolate.

Hot Chocolate

To make one serving:
5 T. Hot Chocolate Mix
6 oz. (3/4 C.) boiling water
Marshmallows, optional

Place the Hot Chocolate Mix in a mug. Pour boiling water over the mixture. Stir until the mix is completely dissolved. If desired, garnish with marshmallows.

Hot Chocolate

To make one serving:
5 T. Hot Chocolate Mix
6 oz. (3/4 C.) boiling water

Marshmallows, optional

   Place the Hot Chocolate Mix in a mug. Pour boiling water over
the mixture. Stir until the mix is completely dissolved. If desired,
garnish with marshmallows.

Hot Chocolate

To make one serving:
5 T. Hot Chocolate Mix
6 oz. (3/4 C.) boiling water

Marshmallows, optional

   Place the Hot Chocolate Mix in a mug. Pour boiling water over
the mixture. Stir until the mix is completely dissolved. If desired,
garnish with marshmallows.

Hot Chocolate

To make one serving:
5 T. Hot Chocolate Mix
6 oz. (3/4 C.) boiling water

Marshmallows, optional

   Place the Hot Chocolate Mix in a mug. Pour boiling water over
the mixture. Stir until the mix is completely dissolved. If desired,
garnish with marshmallows.

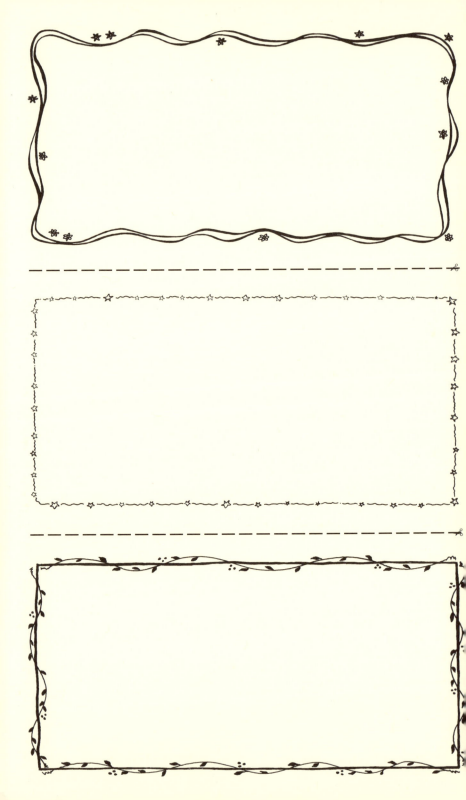

Hot Chocolate

To make one serving:
5 T. Hot Chocolate Mix   Marshmallows, optional
6 oz. (3/4 C.) boiling water

Place the Hot Chocolate Mix in a mug. Pour boiling water over the mixture. Stir until the mix is completely dissolved. If desired, garnish with marshmallows.

Hot Chocolate

To make one serving:
5 T. Hot Chocolate Mix   Marshmallows, optional
6 oz. (3/4 C.) boiling water

Place the Hot Chocolate Mix in a mug. Pour boiling water over the mixture. Stir until the mix is completely dissolved. If desired, garnish with marshmallows.

Hot Chocolate

To make one serving:
5 T. Hot Chocolate Mix   Marshmallows, optional
6 oz. (3/4 C.) boiling water

Place the Hot Chocolate Mix in a mug. Pour boiling water over the mixture. Stir until the mix is completely dissolved. If desired, garnish with marshmallows.

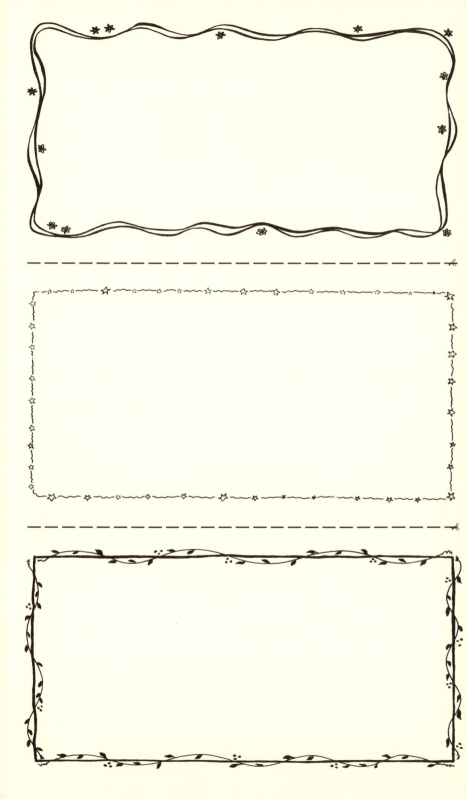

Spiced Mocha Coffee Mix

1 C. instant coffee granules
1 1/2 C. unsweetened cocoa
1 1/2 C. powdered instant dry
   milk
1 T. ground cinnamon
2 T. dried orange peel

In a large bowl, combine the above ingredients and stir until the mixture is well blended. Place mix in a wide-mouth 1-quart canning jar.

Attach a gift tag with the directions on how to prepare the coffee.

Spiced Mocha Coffee

To make one serving:
1 T. Spiced Mocha Coffee Mix
6 oz. (3/4 C.) boiling water
Shaved chocolate, optional

Place the Spiced Mocha Coffee Mix in a mug. Pour boiling water over the mixture. Stir until the mix is completely dissolved. If desired, garnish with shaved chocolate.

Spiced Mocha Coffee

To make one serving:
1 T. Spiced Mocha Coffee Mix   Shaved chocolate, optional
6 oz. (3/4 C.) boiling water

Place the Spiced Mocha Coffee Mix in a mug. Pour boiling water over the mixture. Stir until the mix is completely dissolved. If desired, garnish with shaved chocolate.

Spiced Mocha Coffee

To make one serving:
1 T. Spiced Mocha Coffee Mix   Shaved chocolate, optional
6 oz. (3/4 C.) boiling water

Place the Spiced Mocha Coffee Mix in a mug. Pour boiling water over the mixture. Stir until the mix is completely dissolved. If desired, garnish with shaved chocolate.

Spiced Mocha Coffee

To make one serving:
1 T. Spiced Mocha Coffee Mix   Shaved chocolate, optional
6 oz. (3/4 C.) boiling water

Place the Spiced Mocha Coffee Mix in a mug. Pour boiling water over the mixture. Stir until the mix is completely dissolved. If desired, garnish with shaved chocolate.

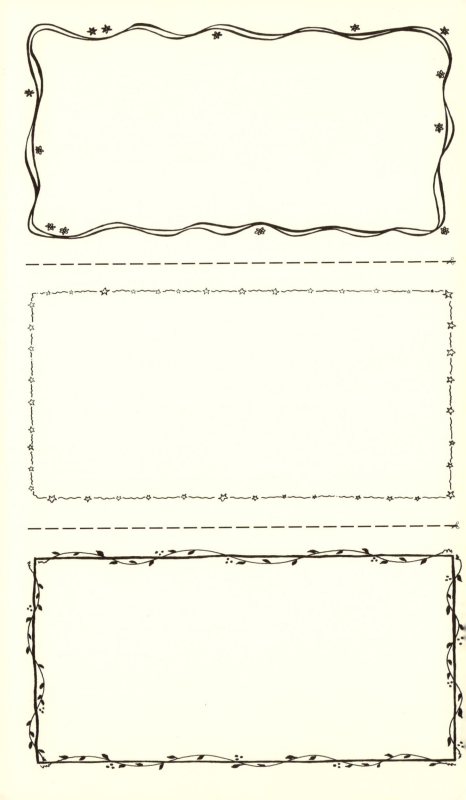

Spiced Mocha Coffee

To make one serving:
1 T. Spiced Mocha Coffee Mix   Shaved chocolate, optional
6 oz. (3/4 C.) boiling water

Place the Spiced Mocha Coffee Mix in a mug. Pour boiling water over the mixture. Stir until the mix is completely dissolved. If desired, garnish with shaved chocolate.

Spiced Mocha Coffee

To make one serving:
1 T. Spiced Mocha Coffee Mix   Shaved chocolate, optional
6 oz. (3/4 C.) boiling water

Place the Spiced Mocha Coffee Mix in a mug. Pour boiling water over the mixture. Stir until the mix is completely dissolved. If desired, garnish with shaved chocolate.

Spiced Mocha Coffee

To make one serving:
1 T. Spiced Mocha Coffee Mix   Shaved chocolate, optional
6 oz. (3/4 C.) boiling water

Place the Spiced Mocha Coffee Mix in a mug. Pour boiling water over the mixture. Stir until the mix is completely dissolved. If desired, garnish with shaved chocolate.

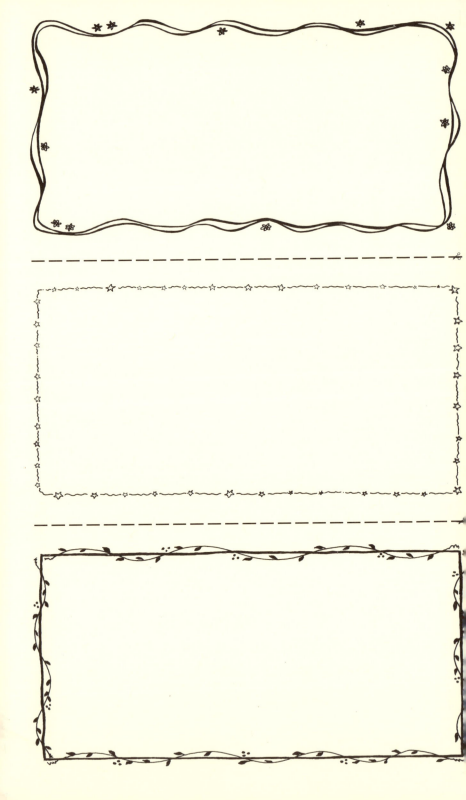

Cappuccino Mix

1 1/4 C. powdered coffee
   creamer
1 1/4 C. powdered chocolate
   flavored drink mix
1 C. plus 2 T. instant coffee
   granules
2/3 C. sugar
1/2 tsp. plus 1/8 tsp. ground
   cinnamon
1/4 tsp. plus 1/8 tsp. ground
   nutmeg

In a large bowl, combine the above ingredients and stir until the mixture is well blended. Place mix in a wide-mouth 1-quart canning jar.

Attach a gift tag with the directions on how to prepare the cappuccino.

❀ *For an out of the ordinary gift, try placing the mix in a mixing bowl along with kitchen utensils, cookbooks, recipe cards, towels and pot holders.* ❀

Cappuccino

To make one serving:
2 T. Cappuccino Mix
6 oz. (3/4 C.) boiling water
Whipped cream and shaved
chocolate, optional

Place the Cappuccino Mix in a mug. Pour boiling water over the mixture. Stir until the mix is completely dissolved. If desired, garnish with whipped cream and shaved chocolate.

Cappuccino

To make one serving:
2 T. Cappuccino Mix
6 oz. (3/4 C.) boiling water

Whipped cream and shaved chocolate, optional

Place the Cappuccino Mix in a mug. Pour boiling water over the mixture. Stir until the mix is completely dissolved. If desired, garnish with whipped cream and shaved chocolate.

Cappuccino

To make one serving:
2 T. Cappuccino Mix
6 oz. (3/4 C.) boiling water

Whipped cream and shaved chocolate, optional

Place the Cappuccino Mix in a mug. Pour boiling water over the mixture. Stir until the mix is completely dissolved. If desired, garnish with whipped cream and shaved chocolate.

Cappuccino

To make one serving:
2 T. Cappuccino Mix
6 oz. (3/4 C.) boiling water

Whipped cream and shaved chocolate, optional

Place the Cappuccino Mix in a mug. Pour boiling water over the mixture. Stir until the mix is completely dissolved. If desired, garnish with whipped cream and shaved chocolate.

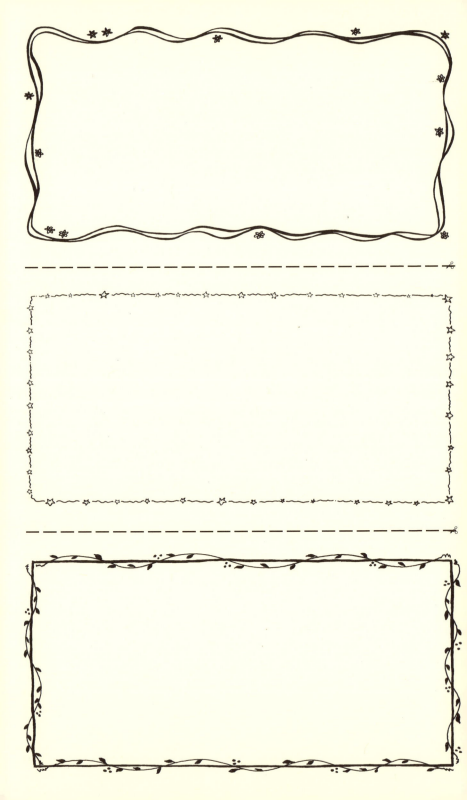

Cappuccino

To make one serving:
2 T. Cappuccino Mix
6 oz. (3/4 C.) boiling water

Whipped cream and shaved
chocolate, optional

    Place the Cappuccino Mix in a mug. Pour boiling water over the mixture. Stir until the mix is completely dissolved. If desired, garnish with whipped cream and shaved chocolate.

Cappuccino

To make one serving:
2 T. Cappuccino Mix
6 oz. (3/4 C.) boiling water

Whipped cream and shaved
chocolate, optional

    Place the Cappuccino Mix in a mug. Pour boiling water over the mixture. Stir until the mix is completely dissolved. If desired, garnish with whipped cream and shaved chocolate.

Cappuccino

To make one serving:
2 T. Cappuccino Mix
6 oz. (3/4 C.) boiling water

Whipped cream and shaved
chocolate, optional

    Place the Cappuccino Mix in a mug. Pour boiling water over the mixture. Stir until the mix is completely dissolved. If desired, garnish with whipped cream and shaved chocolate.

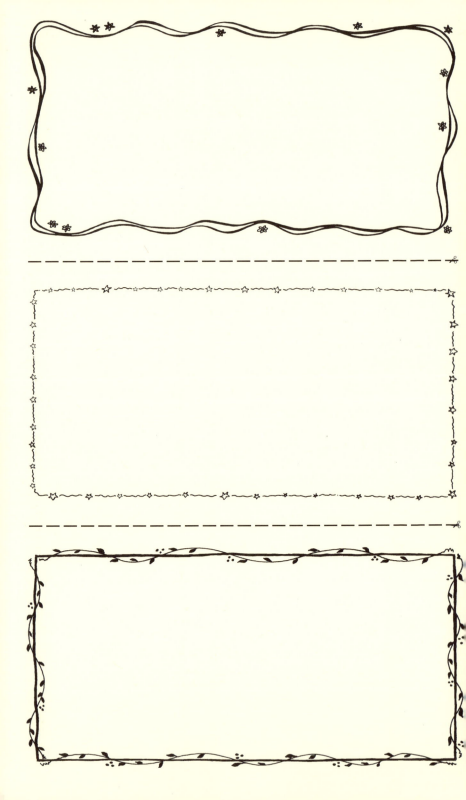

Chocolate Mint Coffee Mix

1 C. plus 2 T. powdered coffee
    creamer
1 1/2 C. sugar
1 C. plus 2 T. instant coffee
    granules
6 T. unsweetened cocoa
9 hard peppermint candies,
    crushed

In a large bowl, combine the above ingredients and stir until the mixture is well blended. Place mix in a wide-mouth 1-quart canning jar.

Attach a gift tag with the directions on how to prepare the coffee.

❀ *For a different look, place a small amount of stuffing under a fabric cover before attaching to "puff" the top.* ❀

Chocolate Mint Coffee

To make one serving:
1 1/2 T. Chocolate Mint Coffee
** Mix**
6 oz. (3/4 C.) boiling water
Whipped cream and candy cane,
** optional**

Place the Chocolate Mint Coffee Mix in a mug. Pour boiling water over the mixture. Stir until the mix is completely dissolved. If desired, garnish with whipped cream and stir drink with a candy cane.

Chocolate Mint Coffee

To make one serving:
1 1/2 T. Chocolate Mint
    Coffee Mix
6 oz. (3/4 C.) boiling water

Whipped cream and candy
    cane, optional

Place the Chocolate Mint Coffee Mix in a mug. Pour boiling water over the mixture. Stir until the mix is completely dissolved. If desired, garnish with whipped cream and stir drink with a candy cane.

Chocolate Mint Coffee

To make one serving:
1 1/2 T. Chocolate Mint
    Coffee Mix
6 oz. (3/4 C.) boiling water

Whipped cream and candy
    cane, optional

Place the Chocolate Mint Coffee Mix in a mug. Pour boiling water over the mixture. Stir until the mix is completely dissolved. If desired, garnish with whipped cream and stir drink with a candy cane.

Chocolate Mint Coffee

To make one serving:
1 1/2 T. Chocolate Mint
    Coffee Mix
6 oz. (3/4 C.) boiling water

Whipped cream and candy
    cane, optional

Place the Chocolate Mint Coffee Mix in a mug. Pour boiling water over the mixture. Stir until the mix is completely dissolved. If desired, garnish with whipped cream and stir drink with a candy cane.

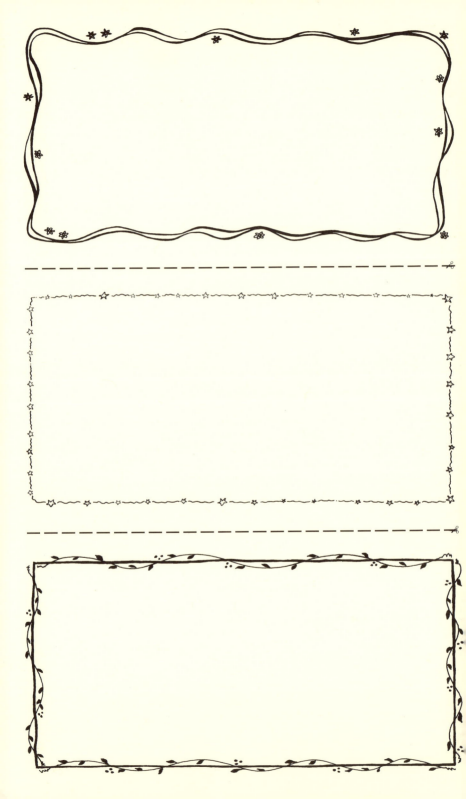

Chocolate Mint Coffee

To make one serving:
1 1/2 T. Chocolate Mint
   Coffee Mix
6 oz. (3/4 C.) boiling water

**Whipped cream and candy
cane, optional**

   Place the Chocolate Mint Coffee Mix in a mug. Pour boiling water over the mixture. Stir until the mix is completely dissolved. If desired, garnish with whipped cream and stir drink with a candy cane.

Chocolate Mint Coffee

To make one serving:
1 1/2 T. Chocolate Mint
   Coffee Mix
6 oz. (3/4 C.) boiling water

**Whipped cream and candy
cane, optional**

   Place the Chocolate Mint Coffee Mix in a mug. Pour boiling water over the mixture. Stir until the mix is completely dissolved. If desired, garnish with whipped cream and stir drink with a candy cane.

Chocolate Mint Coffee

To make one serving:
1 1/2 T. Chocolate Mint
   Coffee Mix
6 oz. (3/4 C.) boiling water

**Whipped cream and candy
cane, optional**

   Place the Chocolate Mint Coffee Mix in a mug. Pour boiling water over the mixture. Stir until the mix is completely dissolved. If desired, garnish with whipped cream and stir drink with a candy cane.

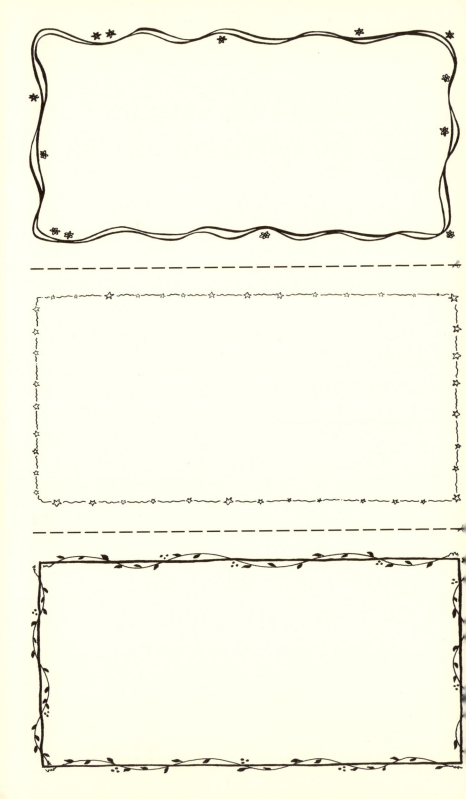

Double Chocolate Hot Cocoa Mix

2/3 C. powdered coffee creamer
2/3 C. milk chocolate chips
2/3 C. powdered sugar
2/3 C. powdered chocolate
    flavored drink mix
2/3 C. powdered instant dry milk
1 1/3 C. miniature marshmallows

In a large bowl, combine the above ingredients and stir until the mixture is well blended. Place mix in a wide-mouth 1-quart canning jar.

Attach a gift tag with the directions on how to prepare the hot cocoa.

❀ *Fill a gift basket with hot drink mixes, marshmallows, chocolate, a big mug and a journal.* ❀

Double Chocolate Hot Cocoa

To make one serving:
2 T. Double Chocolate Hot Cocoa
  Mix
8 oz. (1 C.) boiling water
Marshmallows, optional

Place the Double Chocolate Hot Cocoa Mix in a mug. Pour boiling water over the mixture. Stir until the mix is completely dissolved. If desired, garnish with additional marshmallows.

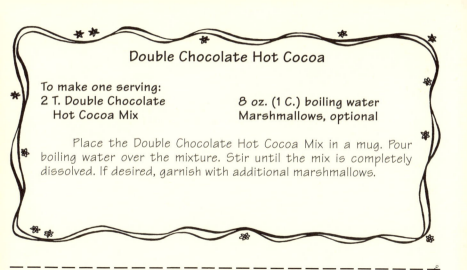

Double Chocolate Hot Cocoa

To make one serving:
2 T. Double Chocolate
   Hot Cocoa Mix

8 oz. (1 C.) boiling water
Marshmallows, optional

    Place the Double Chocolate Hot Cocoa Mix in a mug. Pour boiling water over the mixture. Stir until the mix is completely dissolved. If desired, garnish with additional marshmallows.

Double Chocolate Hot Cocoa

To make one serving:
2 T. Double Chocolate
   Hot Cocoa Mix

8 oz. (1 C.) boiling water
Marshmallows, optional

    Place the Double Chocolate Hot Cocoa Mix in a mug. Pour boiling water over the mixture. Stir until the mix is completely dissolved. If desired, garnish with additional marshmallows.

Double Chocolate Hot Cocoa

To make one serving:
2 T. Double Chocolate
   Hot Cocoa Mix

8 oz. (1 C.) boiling water
Marshmallows, optional

    Place the Double Chocolate Hot Cocoa Mix in a mug. Pour boiling water over the mixture. Stir until the mix is completely dissolved. If desired, garnish with additional marshmallows.

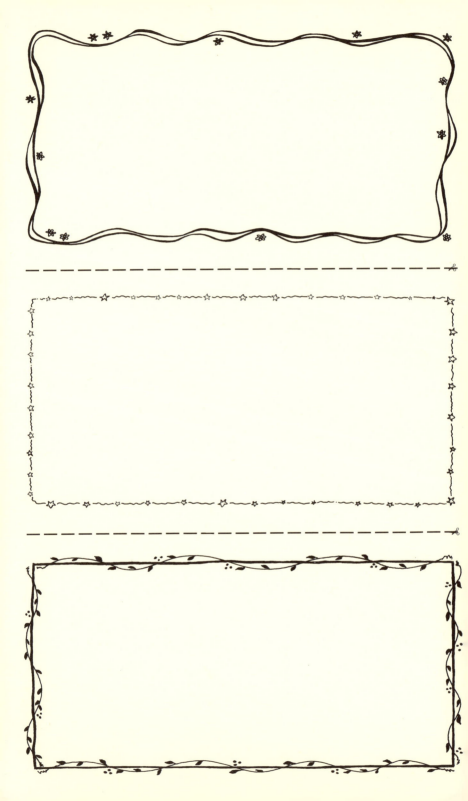

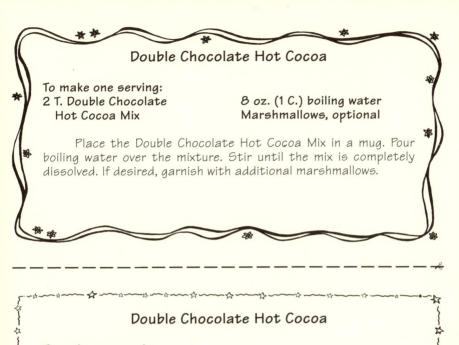

Double Chocolate Hot Cocoa

To make one serving:
2 T. Double Chocolate   8 oz. (1 C.) boiling water
  Hot Cocoa Mix   Marshmallows, optional

Place the Double Chocolate Hot Cocoa Mix in a mug. Pour boiling water over the mixture. Stir until the mix is completely dissolved. If desired, garnish with additional marshmallows.

Double Chocolate Hot Cocoa

To make one serving:
2 T. Double Chocolate   8 oz. (1 C.) boiling water
  Hot Cocoa Mix   Marshmallows, optional

Place the Double Chocolate Hot Cocoa Mix in a mug. Pour boiling water over the mixture. Stir until the mix is completely dissolved. If desired, garnish with additional marshmallows.

Double Chocolate Hot Cocoa

To make one serving:
2 T. Double Chocolate   8 oz. (1 C.) boiling water
  Hot Cocoa Mix   Marshmallows, optional

Place the Double Chocolate Hot Cocoa Mix in a mug. Pour boiling water over the mixture. Stir until the mix is completely dissolved. If desired, garnish with additional marshmallows.

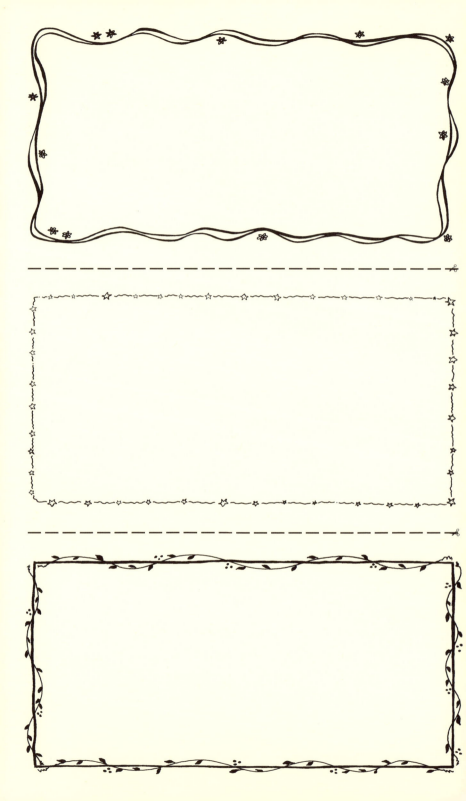

Raspberry Tea Mix

2 large boxes raspberry gelatin
1 1/4 C. sugar
2 tsp. ginger
1 1/4 C. unsweetened instant tea

In a large bowl, combine the above ingredients and stir until the mixture is well blended. Place mix in a wide-mouth 1-quart canning jar.

Attach a gift tag with the directions on how to prepare the tea.

❀ *At times, it may seem impossible to make all of the jar ingredients fit, but with persistence, they do all fit.* ❀

Raspberry Tea

To make one serving:
2 T. Raspberry Tea Mix
8 oz. (1 C.) boiling water or cold
water

Place the Raspberry Tea Mix in a mug. To make hot tea, pour boiling water over the mixture. To make iced tea, pour cold water over the mixture and add ice cubes. Stir until the mix is completely dissolved.

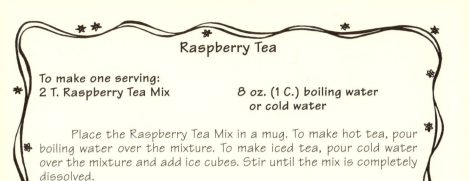

Raspberry Tea

To make one serving:
2 T. Raspberry Tea Mix

8 oz. (1 C.) boiling water
or cold water

Place the Raspberry Tea Mix in a mug. To make hot tea, pour boiling water over the mixture. To make iced tea, pour cold water over the mixture and add ice cubes. Stir until the mix is completely dissolved.

Raspberry Tea

To make one serving:
2 T. Raspberry Tea Mix

8 oz. (1 C.) boiling water
or cold water

Place the Raspberry Tea Mix in a mug. To make hot tea, pour boiling water over the mixture. To make iced tea, pour cold water over the mixture and add ice cubes. Stir until the mix is completely dissolved.

Raspberry Tea

To make one serving:
2 T. Raspberry Tea Mix

8 oz. (1 C.) boiling water
or cold water

Place the Raspberry Tea Mix in a mug. To make hot tea, pour boiling water over the mixture. To make iced tea, pour cold water over the mixture and add ice cubes. Stir until the mix is completely dissolved.

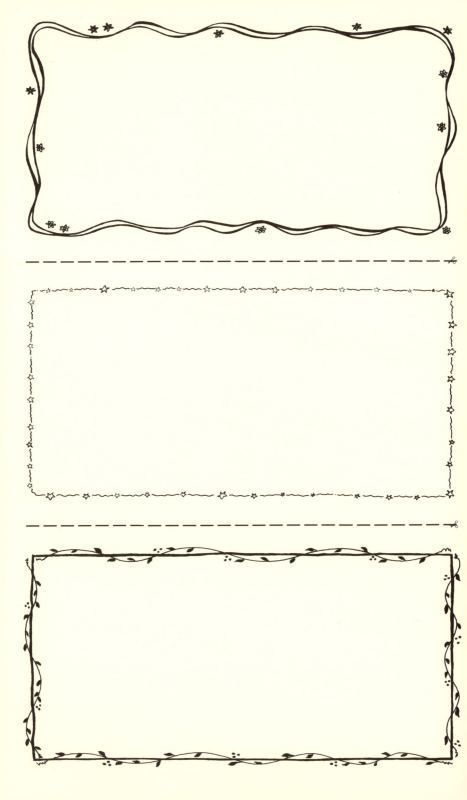

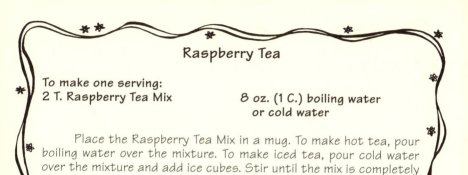

Raspberry Tea

To make one serving:
2 T. Raspberry Tea Mix

8 oz. (1 C.) boiling water
or cold water

Place the Raspberry Tea Mix in a mug. To make hot tea, pour boiling water over the mixture. To make iced tea, pour cold water over the mixture and add ice cubes. Stir until the mix is completely dissolved.

Raspberry Tea

To make one serving:
2 T. Raspberry Tea Mix

8 oz. (1 C.) boiling water
or cold water

Place the Raspberry Tea Mix in a mug. To make hot tea, pour boiling water over the mixture. To make iced tea, pour cold water over the mixture and add ice cubes. Stir until the mix is completely dissolved.

Raspberry Tea

To make one serving:
2 T. Raspberry Tea Mix

8 oz. (1 C.) boiling water
or cold water

Place the Raspberry Tea Mix in a mug. To make hot tea, pour boiling water over the mixture. To make iced tea, pour cold water over the mixture and add ice cubes. Stir until the mix is completely dissolved.

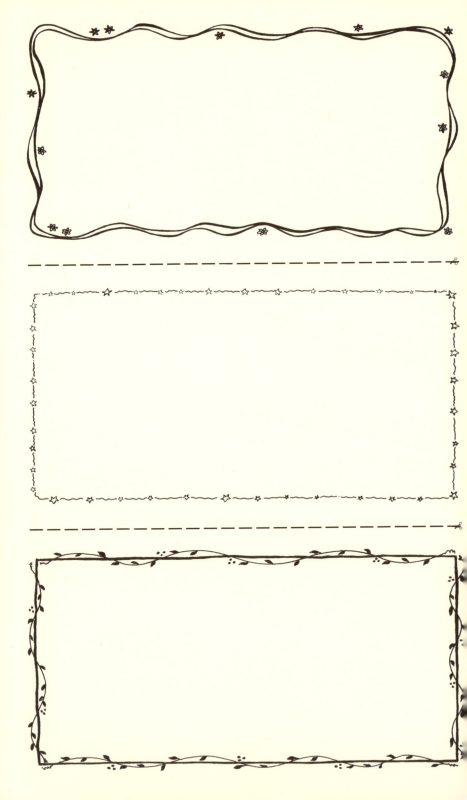

Swiss Mocha Mix

1 C. instant coffee granules
1 C. sugar
2 C. powdered instant dry milk
4 tsp. unsweetened cocoa

In a large bowl, combine the above ingredients and stir until the mixture is well blended. Place mix in a wide-mouth 1-quart canning jar.

Attach a gift tag with the directions on how to prepare the mocha.

Swiss Mocha

To make one serving:
2 tsp. Swiss Mocha Mix
8 oz. (1 C.) boiling water
Whipped cream, optional

Place the Swiss Mocha Mix in a mug. Pour boiling water over the mixture. Stir until the mix is completely dissolved. If desired, garnish with whipped cream.

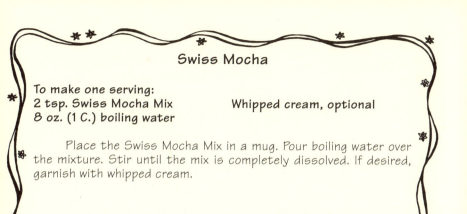

Swiss Mocha

To make one serving:
2 tsp. Swiss Mocha Mix
8 oz. (1 C.) boiling water

Whipped cream, optional

Place the Swiss Mocha Mix in a mug. Pour boiling water over the mixture. Stir until the mix is completely dissolved. If desired, garnish with whipped cream.

Swiss Mocha

To make one serving:
2 tsp. Swiss Mocha Mix
8 oz. (1 C.) boiling water

Whipped cream, optional

Place the Swiss Mocha Mix in a mug. Pour boiling water over the mixture. Stir until the mix is completely dissolved. If desired, garnish with whipped cream.

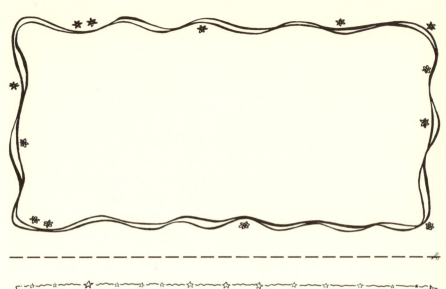

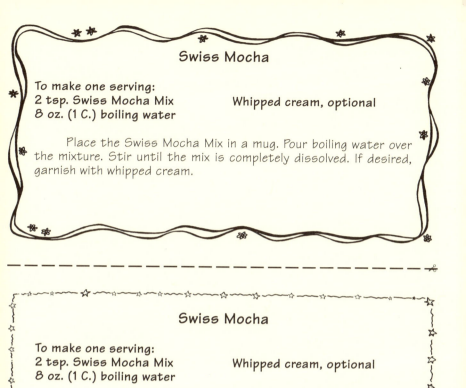

Swiss Mocha

To make one serving:
2 tsp. Swiss Mocha Mix
8 oz. (1 C.) boiling water

Whipped cream, optional

Place the Swiss Mocha Mix in a mug. Pour boiling water over the mixture. Stir until the mix is completely dissolved. If desired, garnish with whipped cream.

Swiss Mocha

To make one serving:
2 tsp. Swiss Mocha Mix
8 oz. (1 C.) boiling water

Whipped cream, optional

Place the Swiss Mocha Mix in a mug. Pour boiling water over the mixture. Stir until the mix is completely dissolved. If desired, garnish with whipped cream.

Swiss Mocha

To make one serving:
2 tsp. Swiss Mocha Mix
8 oz. (1 C.) boiling water

Whipped cream, optional

Place the Swiss Mocha Mix in a mug. Pour boiling water over the mixture. Stir until the mix is completely dissolved. If desired, garnish with whipped cream.

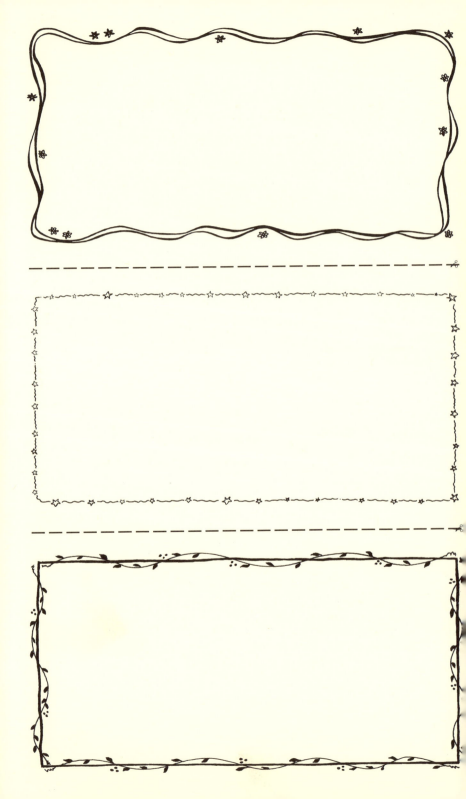

Friendship Tea Mix

1 (15 oz.) jar powdered orange
    flavored drink mix
1 C. sugar
1/2 C. presweetened lemonade
    mix
1/2 C. unsweetened instant tea
1 small box apricot flavored
    gelatin
2 1/2 tsp. ground cinnamon
1 tsp. ground cloves

In a large bowl, combine the above
ingredients and stir until the mixture is well
blended. Place mix in a wide-mouth 1-quart
canning jar.

Attach a gift tag with the directions on
how to prepare the tea.

❀ *Small appliques or embroidery can be
added to the center of a fabric cover to
further personalize the gift.* ❀

Friendship Tea

To make one serving:
1 1/2 T. Friendship Tea Mix
8 oz. (1 C.) boiling water

Place the Friendship Tea Mix in a mug. Pour boiling water over the mixture. Stir until the mix is completely dissolved.

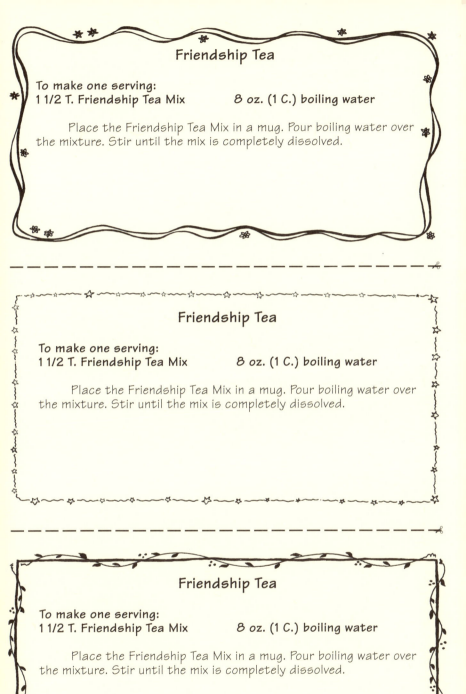

Friendship Tea

To make one serving:
1 1/2 T. Friendship Tea Mix   8 oz. (1 C.) boiling water

 Place the Friendship Tea Mix in a mug. Pour boiling water over the mixture. Stir until the mix is completely dissolved.

Friendship Tea

To make one serving:
1 1/2 T. Friendship Tea Mix   8 oz. (1 C.) boiling water

 Place the Friendship Tea Mix in a mug. Pour boiling water over the mixture. Stir until the mix is completely dissolved.

Friendship Tea

To make one serving:
1 1/2 T. Friendship Tea Mix   8 oz. (1 C.) boiling water

 Place the Friendship Tea Mix in a mug. Pour boiling water over the mixture. Stir until the mix is completely dissolved.

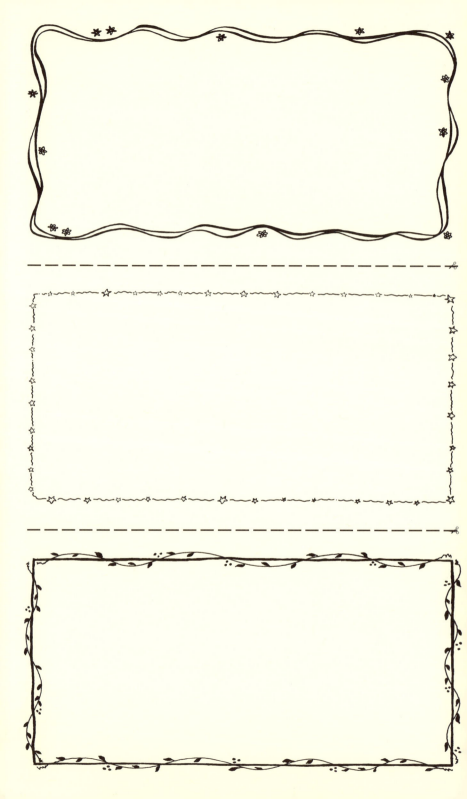

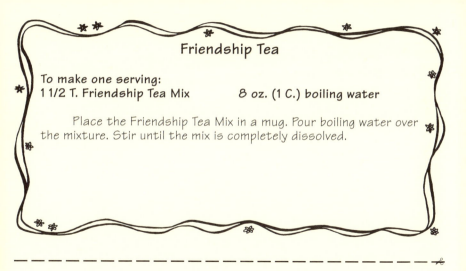

Friendship Tea

To make one serving:
1 1/2 T. Friendship Tea Mix   8 oz. (1 C.) boiling water

Place the Friendship Tea Mix in a mug. Pour boiling water over the mixture. Stir until the mix is completely dissolved.

Friendship Tea

To make one serving:
1 1/2 T. Friendship Tea Mix   8 oz. (1 C.) boiling water

Place the Friendship Tea Mix in a mug. Pour boiling water over the mixture. Stir until the mix is completely dissolved.

Friendship Tea

To make one serving:
1 1/2 T. Friendship Tea Mix   8 oz. (1 C.) boiling water

Place the Friendship Tea Mix in a mug. Pour boiling water over the mixture. Stir until the mix is completely dissolved.

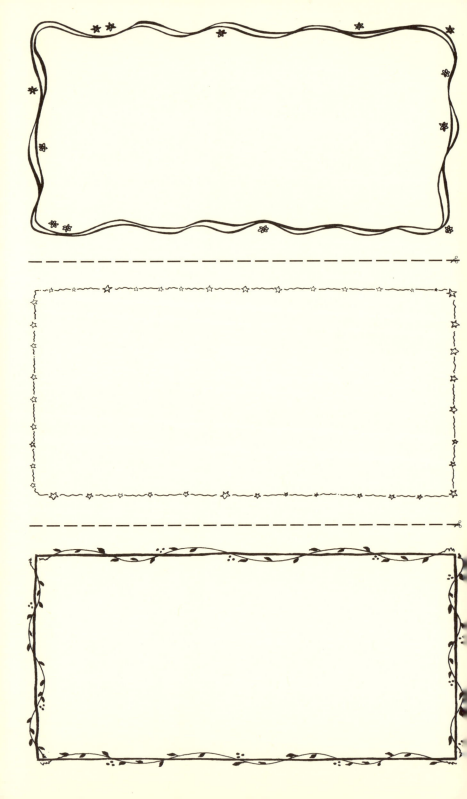

Mocha Coffee Mix

5 T. instant coffee granules
1 3/4 C. powdered instant dry
  milk
1 1/2 C. powdered chocolate
  flavored drink mix
1 T. powdered sugar
7 T. powdered coffee creamer

In a large bowl, combine the above ingredients and stir until the mixture is well blended. Place mix in a wide-mouth 1-quart canning jar.

Attach a gift tag with the directions on how to prepare the coffee.

Mocha Coffee

To make one serving:
4 T. Mocha Coffee Mix
8 oz. (1 C.) boiling water
Whipped cream and shaved
chocolate, optional

Place the Mocha Coffee Mix in a mug. Pour boiling water over the mixture. Stir until the mix is completely dissolved. If desired, garnish with whipped cream and shaved chocolate.

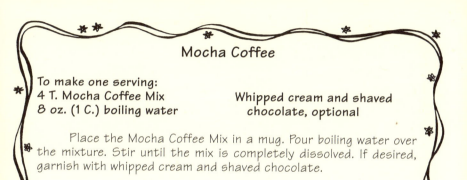

Mocha Coffee

To make one serving:
4 T. Mocha Coffee Mix
8 oz. (1 C.) boiling water

Whipped cream and shaved chocolate, optional

Place the Mocha Coffee Mix in a mug. Pour boiling water over the mixture. Stir until the mix is completely dissolved. If desired, garnish with whipped cream and shaved chocolate.

Mocha Coffee

To make one serving:
4 T. Mocha Coffee Mix
8 oz. (1 C.) boiling water

Whipped cream and shaved chocolate, optional

Place the Mocha Coffee Mix in a mug. Pour boiling water over the mixture. Stir until the mix is completely dissolved. If desired, garnish with whipped cream and shaved chocolate.

Mocha Coffee

To make one serving:
4 T. Mocha Coffee Mix
8 oz. (1 C.) boiling water

Whipped cream and shaved chocolate, optional

Place the Mocha Coffee Mix in a mug. Pour boiling water over the mixture. Stir until the mix is completely dissolved. If desired, garnish with whipped cream and shaved chocolate.

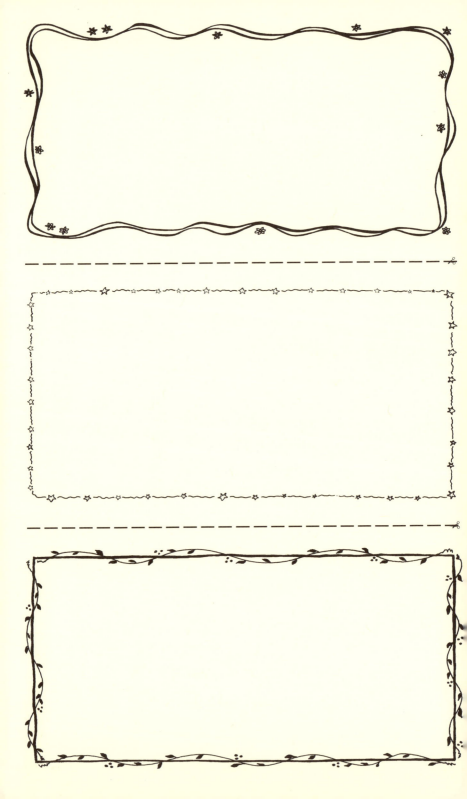

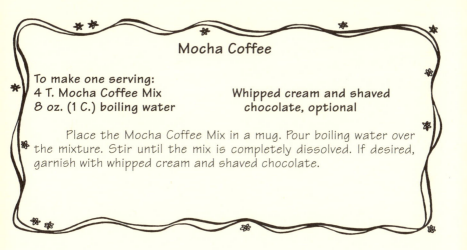

Mocha Coffee

To make one serving:
4 T. Mocha Coffee Mix
8 oz. (1 C.) boiling water

Whipped cream and shaved
chocolate, optional

Place the Mocha Coffee Mix in a mug. Pour boiling water over the mixture. Stir until the mix is completely dissolved. If desired, garnish with whipped cream and shaved chocolate.

Mocha Coffee

To make one serving:
4 T. Mocha Coffee Mix
8 oz. (1 C.) boiling water

Whipped cream and shaved
chocolate, optional

Place the Mocha Coffee Mix in a mug. Pour boiling water over the mixture. Stir until the mix is completely dissolved. If desired, garnish with whipped cream and shaved chocolate.

Mocha Coffee

To make one serving:
4 T. Mocha Coffee Mix
8 oz. (1 C.) boiling water

Whipped cream and shaved
chocolate, optional

Place the Mocha Coffee Mix in a mug. Pour boiling water over the mixture. Stir until the mix is completely dissolved. If desired, garnish with whipped cream and shaved chocolate.

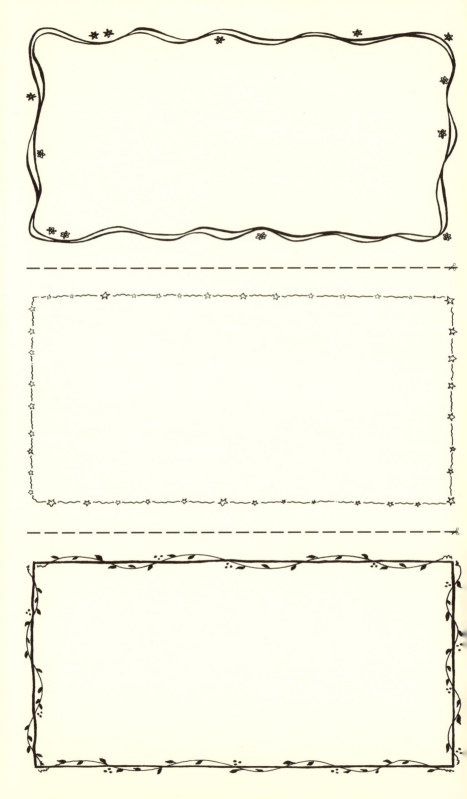

Gourmet Hot Chocolate Mix

1 1/2 C. plus 1 T. powdered
   instant dry milk
1 C. powdered coffee creamer
1 C. powdered chocolate
   flavored drink mix
3/4 C. powdered chocolate
   malted milk flavored drink mix
1/2 C. powdered sugar

In a large bowl, combine the above ingredients and stir until the mixture is well blended. Place mix in a wide-mouth 1-quart canning jar.

Attach a gift tag with the directions on how to prepare the hot chocolate.

Gourmet Hot Chocolate

To make one serving:
3 T. Gourmet Hot Chocolate
 Mix
8 oz. (1 C.) boiling water
Marshmallows or whipped
 cream, optional

Place the Gourmet Hot Chocolate Mix in a mug. Pour boiling water over the mixture. Stir until the mix is completely dissolved. If desired, garnish with marshmallows or whipped cream.

Gourmet Hot Chocolate

To make one serving:
3 T. Gourmet Hot
    Chocolate Mix
8 oz. (1 C.) boiling water

Marshmallows or whipped
cream, optional

Place the Gourmet Hot Chocolate Mix in a mug. Pour boiling water over the mixture. Stir until the mix is completely dissolved. If desired, garnish with marshmallows or whipped cream.

Gourmet Hot Chocolate

To make one serving:
3 T. Gourmet Hot
    Chocolate Mix
8 oz. (1 C.) boiling water

Marshmallows or whipped
cream, optional

Place the Gourmet Hot Chocolate Mix in a mug. Pour boiling water over the mixture. Stir until the mix is completely dissolved. If desired, garnish with marshmallows or whipped cream.

Gourmet Hot Chocolate

To make one serving:
3 T. Gourmet Hot
    Chocolate Mix
8 oz. (1 C.) boiling water

Marshmallows or whipped
cream, optional

Place the Gourmet Hot Chocolate Mix in a mug. Pour boiling water over the mixture. Stir until the mix is completely dissolved. If desired, garnish with marshmallows or whipped cream.

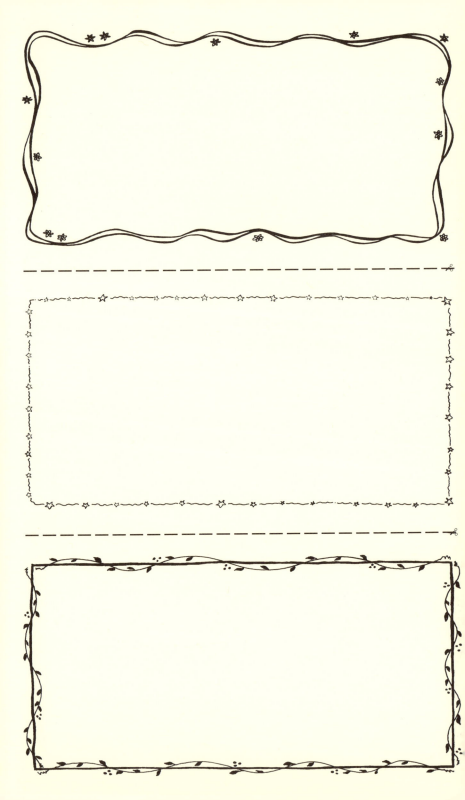

Gourmet Hot Chocolate

To make one serving:
3 T. Gourmet Hot
Chocolate Mix
8 oz. (1 C.) boiling water

Marshmallows or whipped
cream, optional

Place the Gourmet Hot Chocolate Mix in a mug. Pour boiling water over the mixture. Stir until the mix is completely dissolved. If desired, garnish with marshmallows or whipped cream.

Gourmet Hot Chocolate

To make one serving:
3 T. Gourmet Hot
Chocolate Mix
8 oz. (1 C.) boiling water

Marshmallows or whipped
cream, optional

Place the Gourmet Hot Chocolate Mix in a mug. Pour boiling water over the mixture. Stir until the mix is completely dissolved. If desired, garnish with marshmallows or whipped cream.

Gourmet Hot Chocolate

To make one serving:
3 T. Gourmet Hot
Chocolate Mix
8 oz. (1 C.) boiling water

Marshmallows or whipped
cream, optional

Place the Gourmet Hot Chocolate Mix in a mug. Pour boiling water over the mixture. Stir until the mix is completely dissolved. If desired, garnish with marshmallows or whipped cream.

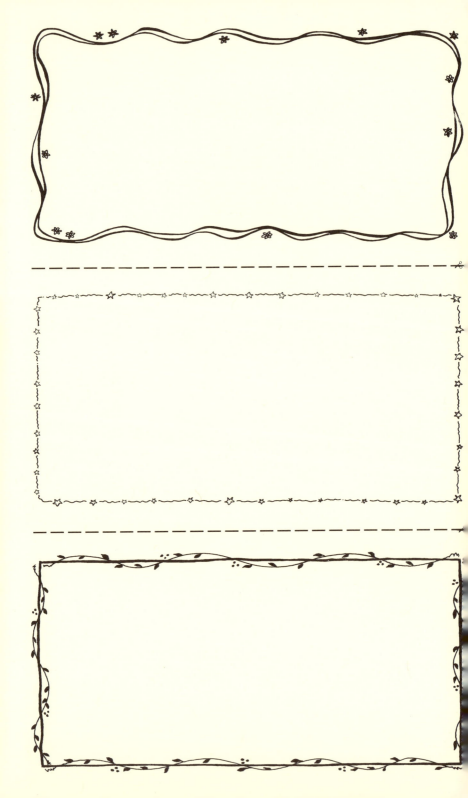

Toffee Coffee Mix

1 1/3 C. instant coffee granules
2 C. powdered coffee creamer
2 C. brown sugar

In a large bowl, combine the above ingredients and stir until the mixture is well blended. Place mix in a wide-mouth 1-quart canning jar.

Attach a gift tag with the directions on how to prepare the coffee.

❀ *For a special touch, attach a wooden spoon to the jar.* ❀

Toffee Coffee

To make one serving:
1 T. Toffee Coffee Mix
8 oz. (1 C.) boiling water

Place the Toffee Coffee Mix in a mug. Pour boiling water over the mixture. Stir until the mix is completely dissolved.

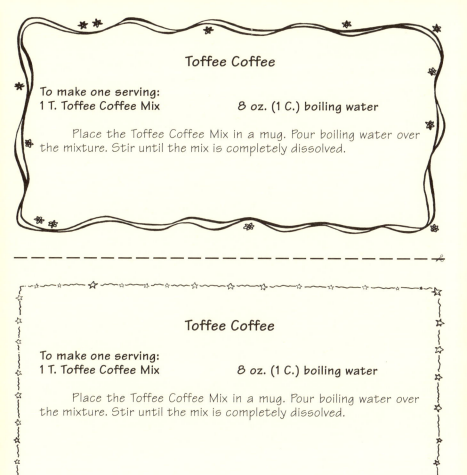

Toffee Coffee

To make one serving:
1 T. Toffee Coffee Mix   8 oz. (1 C.) boiling water

Place the Toffee Coffee Mix in a mug. Pour boiling water over the mixture. Stir until the mix is completely dissolved.

Toffee Coffee

To make one serving:
1 T. Toffee Coffee Mix   8 oz. (1 C.) boiling water

Place the Toffee Coffee Mix in a mug. Pour boiling water over the mixture. Stir until the mix is completely dissolved.

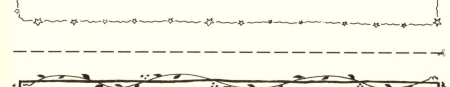

Toffee Coffee

To make one serving:
1 T. Toffee Coffee Mix   8 oz. (1 C.) boiling water

Place the Toffee Coffee Mix in a mug. Pour boiling water over the mixture. Stir until the mix is completely dissolved.

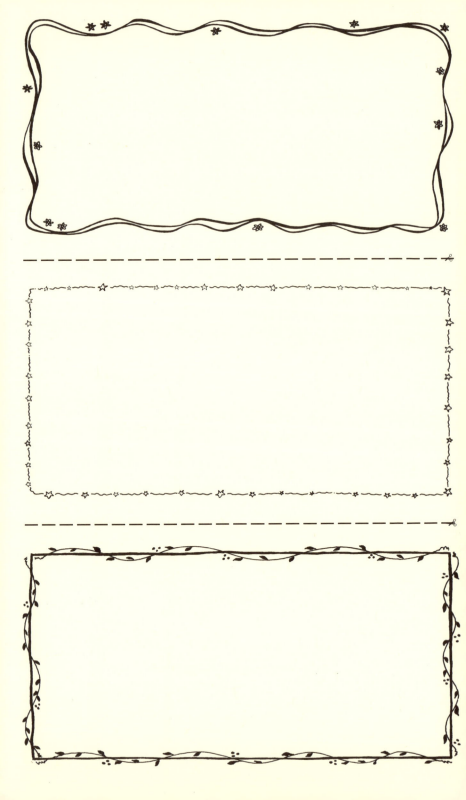

Toffee Coffee

To make one serving:
1 T. Toffee Coffee Mix   **8 oz. (1 C.) boiling water**

Place the Toffee Coffee Mix in a mug. Pour boiling water over the mixture. Stir until the mix is completely dissolved.

Toffee Coffee

To make one serving:
1 T. Toffee Coffee Mix   **8 oz. (1 C.) boiling water**

Place the Toffee Coffee Mix in a mug. Pour boiling water over the mixture. Stir until the mix is completely dissolved.

Toffee Coffee

To make one serving:
1 T. Toffee Coffee Mix   **8 oz. (1 C.) boiling water**

Place the Toffee Coffee Mix in a mug. Pour boiling water over the mixture. Stir until the mix is completely dissolved.

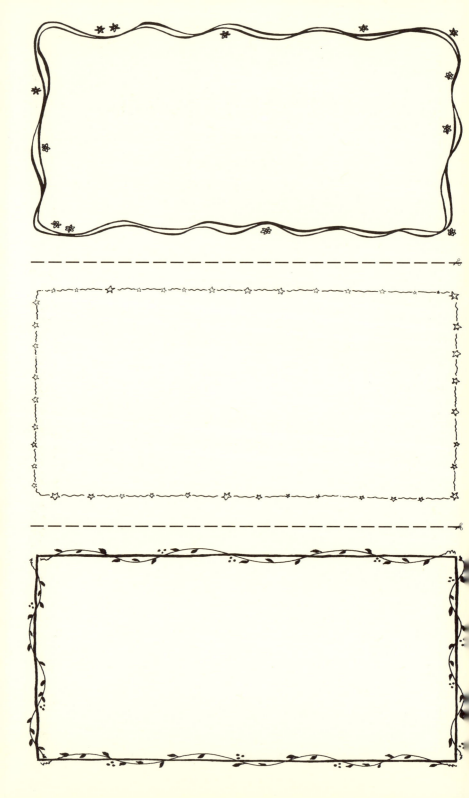

Caribbean Tea Mix

2 C. unsweetened instant tea
1 large package orange-pineapple
   gelatin
1 C. sugar
3/4 tsp. imitation coconut
   extract

In a large bowl, combine the above ingredients and stir until the mixture is well blended. Place mix in a wide-mouth 1-quart canning jar.

Attach a gift tag with the directions on how to prepare the tea.

Caribbean Tea

To make one serving:
1 T. Caribbean Tea Mix
6 oz. (3/4 C.) boiling water

Place the Caribbean Tea Mix in a mug. Pour boiling water over the mixture. Stir until the mix is completely dissolved.

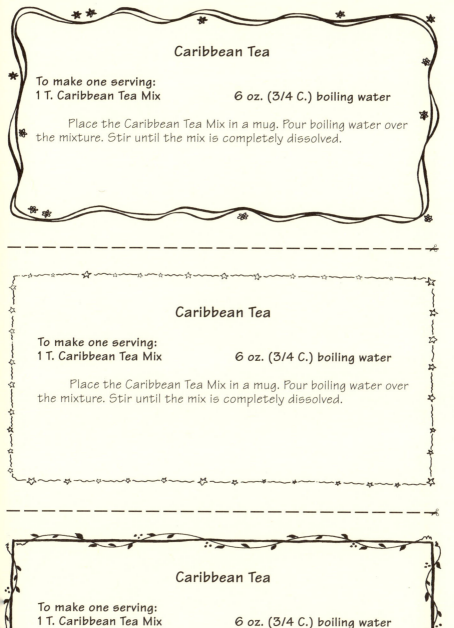

Caribbean Tea

To make one serving:
1 T. Caribbean Tea Mix   **6 oz. (3/4 C.) boiling water**

Place the Caribbean Tea Mix in a mug. Pour boiling water over the mixture. Stir until the mix is completely dissolved.

Caribbean Tea

To make one serving:
1 T. Caribbean Tea Mix   **6 oz. (3/4 C.) boiling water**

Place the Caribbean Tea Mix in a mug. Pour boiling water over the mixture. Stir until the mix is completely dissolved.

Caribbean Tea

To make one serving:
1 T. Caribbean Tea Mix   **6 oz. (3/4 C.) boiling water**

Place the Caribbean Tea Mix in a mug. Pour boiling water over the mixture. Stir until the mix is completely dissolved.

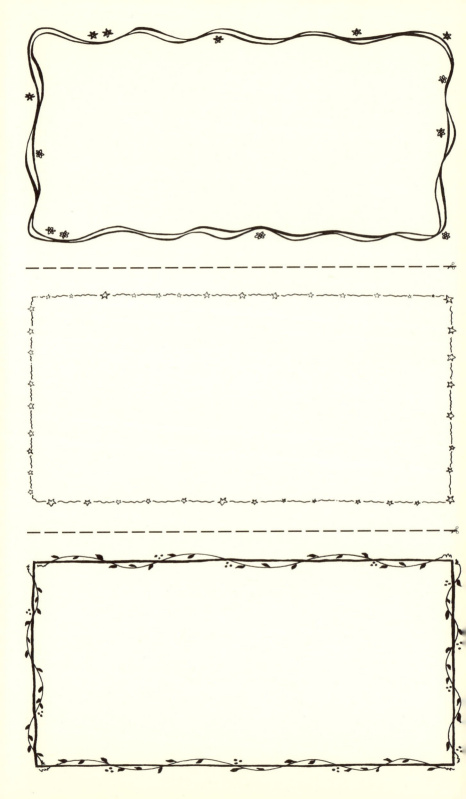

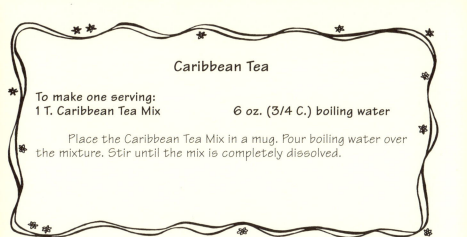

Caribbean Tea

To make one serving:
1 T. Caribbean Tea Mix   6 oz. (3/4 C.) boiling water

Place the Caribbean Tea Mix in a mug. Pour boiling water over the mixture. Stir until the mix is completely dissolved.

Caribbean Tea

To make one serving:
1 T. Caribbean Tea Mix   6 oz. (3/4 C.) boiling water

Place the Caribbean Tea Mix in a mug. Pour boiling water over the mixture. Stir until the mix is completely dissolved.

Caribbean Tea

To make one serving:
1 T. Caribbean Tea Mix   6 oz. (3/4 C.) boiling water

Place the Caribbean Tea Mix in a mug. Pour boiling water over the mixture. Stir until the mix is completely dissolved.

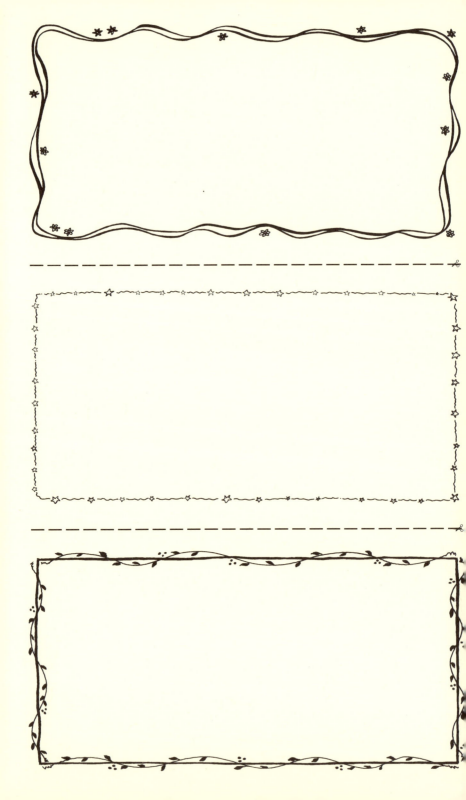

Red Hot Tea Mix

2 C. powdered orange flavored
   drink mix
1 1/2 C. sugar
1/2 C. unsweetened instant tea
2 T. presweetened lemonade
   mix
1/2 C. red hot candies

In a large bowl, combine the above ingredients and stir until the mixture is well blended. Place mix in a wide-mouth 1-quart canning jar.

Attach a gift tag with the directions on how to prepare the tea.

Red Hot Tea

To make one serving:
3 T. Red Hot Tea Mix
8 oz. (1 C.) boiling water

Place the Red Hot Tea Mix in a mug. Pour boiling water over the mixture. Stir until the mix is completely dissolved.

Red Hot Tea

To make one serving:
3 T. Red Hot Tea Mix   8 oz. (1 C.) boiling water

Place the Red Hot Tea Mix in a mug. Pour boiling water over the mixture. Stir until the mix is completely dissolved.

Red Hot Tea

To make one serving:
3 T. Red Hot Tea Mix   8 oz. (1 C.) boiling water

Place the Red Hot Tea Mix in a mug. Pour boiling water over the mixture. Stir until the mix is completely dissolved.

Red Hot Tea

To make one serving:
3 T. Red Hot Tea Mix   8 oz. (1 C.) boiling water

Place the Red Hot Tea Mix in a mug. Pour boiling water over the mixture. Stir until the mix is completely dissolved.

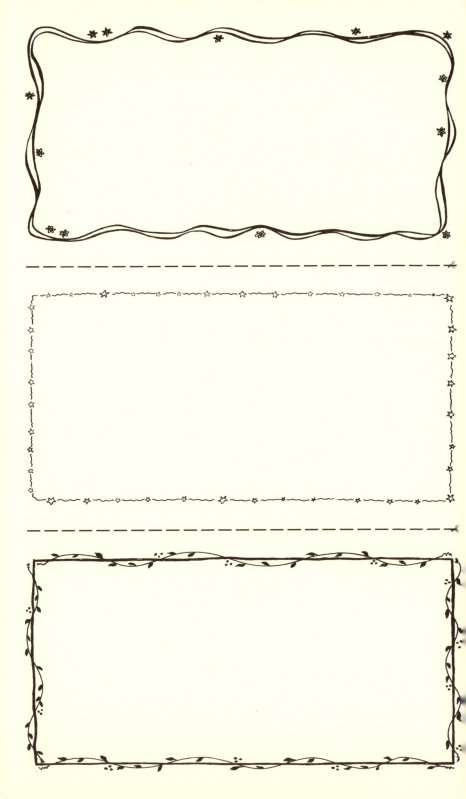

Red Hot Tea

To make one serving:
3 T. Red Hot Tea Mix   **8 oz. (1 C.) boiling water**

Place the Red Hot Tea Mix in a mug. Pour boiling water over the mixture. Stir until the mix is completely dissolved.

Red Hot Tea

To make one serving:
3 T. Red Hot Tea Mix   **8 oz. (1 C.) boiling water**

Place the Red Hot Tea Mix in a mug. Pour boiling water over the mixture. Stir until the mix is completely dissolved.

Red Hot Tea

To make one serving:
3 T. Red Hot Tea Mix   **8 oz. (1 C.) boiling water**

Place the Red Hot Tea Mix in a mug. Pour boiling water over the mixture. Stir until the mix is completely dissolved.

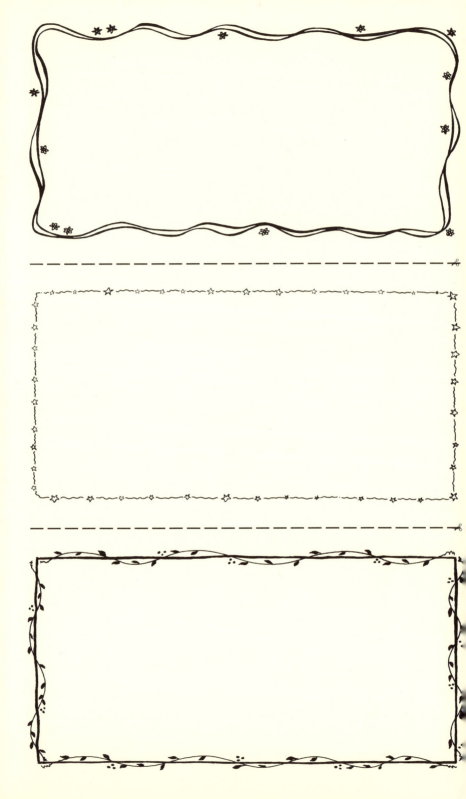

Cinnamon Spice Coffee Mix

1 1/3 C. instant coffee granules
2 2/3 C. sugar
4 tsp. ground cinnamon
1 tsp. ground nutmeg
1/2 tsp. allspice

In a large bowl, combine the above ingredients and stir until the mixture is well blended. Place mix in a wide-mouth 1-quart canning jar.

Attach a gift tag with the directions on how to prepare the coffee.

Cinnamon Spice Coffee

To make one serving:
1 T. Cinnamon Spice Coffee Mix
8 oz. (1 C.) boiling water

Place the Cinnamon Spice Coffee Mix in a mug. Pour boiling water over the mixture. Stir until the mix is completely dissolved.

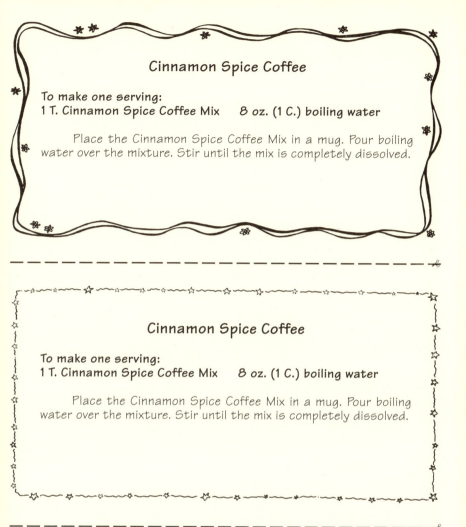

Cinnamon Spice Coffee

To make one serving:
1 T. Cinnamon Spice Coffee Mix   8 oz. (1 C.) boiling water

Place the Cinnamon Spice Coffee Mix in a mug. Pour boiling water over the mixture. Stir until the mix is completely dissolved.

Cinnamon Spice Coffee

To make one serving:
1 T. Cinnamon Spice Coffee Mix   8 oz. (1 C.) boiling water

Place the Cinnamon Spice Coffee Mix in a mug. Pour boiling water over the mixture. Stir until the mix is completely dissolved.

Cinnamon Spice Coffee

To make one serving:
1 T. Cinnamon Spice Coffee Mix   8 oz. (1 C.) boiling water

Place the Cinnamon Spice Coffee Mix in a mug. Pour boiling water over the mixture. Stir until the mix is completely dissolved.

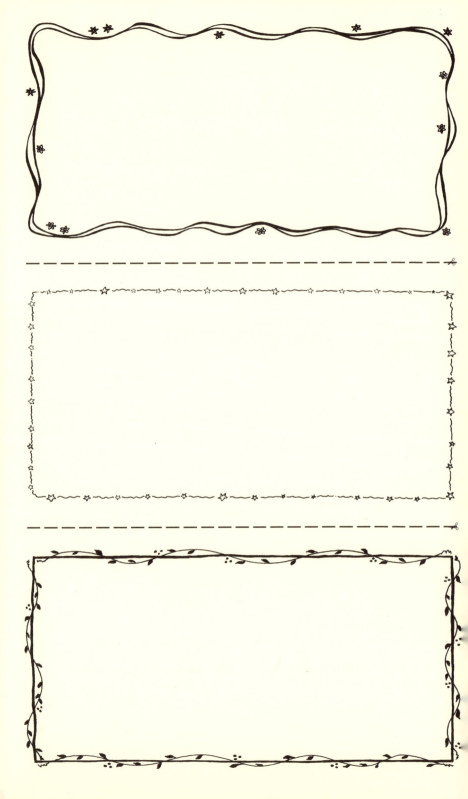

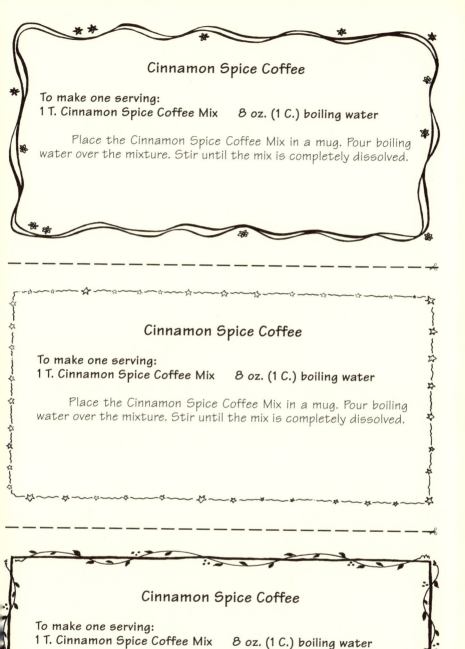

Cinnamon Spice Coffee

To make one serving:
1 T. Cinnamon Spice Coffee Mix   8 oz. (1 C.) boiling water

Place the Cinnamon Spice Coffee Mix in a mug. Pour boiling water over the mixture. Stir until the mix is completely dissolved.

Cinnamon Spice Coffee

To make one serving:
1 T. Cinnamon Spice Coffee Mix   8 oz. (1 C.) boiling water

Place the Cinnamon Spice Coffee Mix in a mug. Pour boiling water over the mixture. Stir until the mix is completely dissolved.

Cinnamon Spice Coffee

To make one serving:
1 T. Cinnamon Spice Coffee Mix   8 oz. (1 C.) boiling water

Place the Cinnamon Spice Coffee Mix in a mug. Pour boiling water over the mixture. Stir until the mix is completely dissolved.

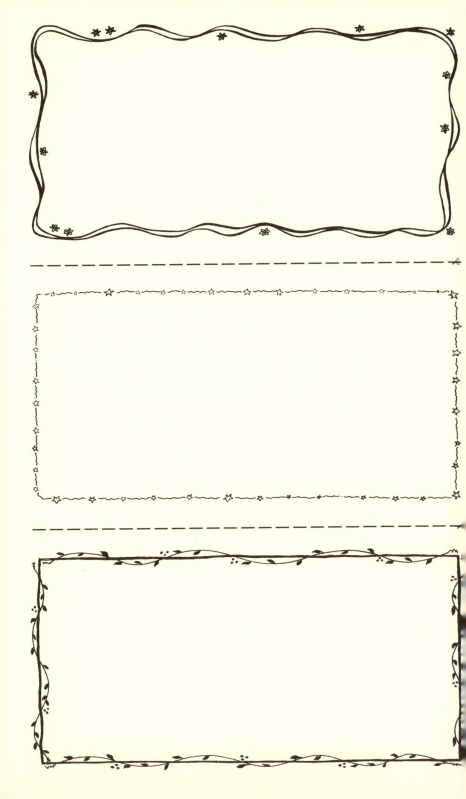

Night Cap Coffee Mix

2 C. powdered coffee creamer
1 C. instant coffee granules
1 C. sugar
2 tsp. ground cardamom
1 1/2 tsp. ground cinnamon

In a large bowl, combine the above ingredients and stir until the mixture is well blended. Place mix in a wide-mouth 1-quart canning jar.

Attach a gift tag with the directions on how to prepare the coffee.

❀ To make a gift in a jar fancier, decorate it with a doily and ribbon. ❀

Night Cap Coffee

To make one serving:
1 heaping T. Night Cap Coffee
Mix
8 oz. (1 C.) boiling water

Place the Night Cap Coffee Mix in a mug. Pour boiling water over the mixture. Stir until the mix is completely dissolved.

Night Cap Coffee

To make one serving:
1 heaping T. Night Cap Coffee   8 oz. (1 C.) boiling water
   Mix

   Place the Night Cap Coffee Mix in a mug. Pour boiling water over the mixture. Stir until the mix is completely dissolved.

Night Cap Coffee

To make one serving:
1 heaping T. Night Cap Coffee   8 oz. (1 C.) boiling water
   Mix

   Place the Night Cap Coffee Mix in a mug. Pour boiling water over the mixture. Stir until the mix is completely dissolved.

Night Cap Coffee

To make one serving:
1 heaping T. Night Cap Coffee   8 oz. (1 C.) boiling water
   Mix

   Place the Night Cap Coffee Mix in a mug. Pour boiling water over the mixture. Stir until the mix is completely dissolved.

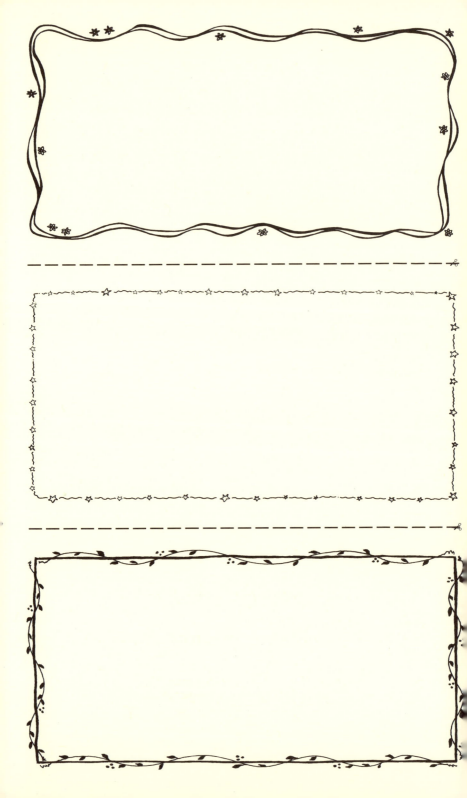

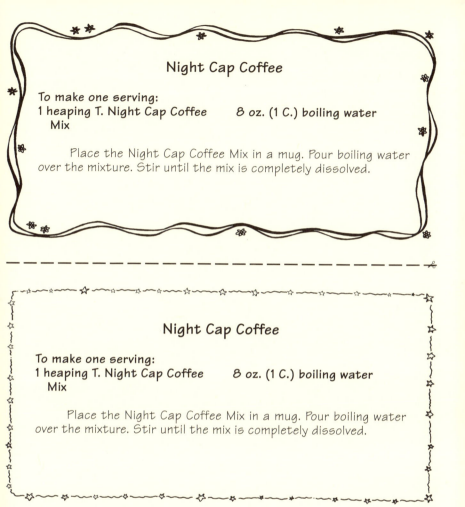

Night Cap Coffee

To make one serving:
1 heaping T. Night Cap Coffee   8 oz. (1 C.) boiling water
   Mix

   Place the Night Cap Coffee Mix in a mug. Pour boiling water over the mixture. Stir until the mix is completely dissolved.

Night Cap Coffee

To make one serving:
1 heaping T. Night Cap Coffee   8 oz. (1 C.) boiling water
   Mix

   Place the Night Cap Coffee Mix in a mug. Pour boiling water over the mixture. Stir until the mix is completely dissolved.

Night Cap Coffee

To make one serving:
1 heaping T. Night Cap Coffee   8 oz. (1 C.) boiling water
   Mix

   Place the Night Cap Coffee Mix in a mug. Pour boiling water over the mixture. Stir until the mix is completely dissolved.

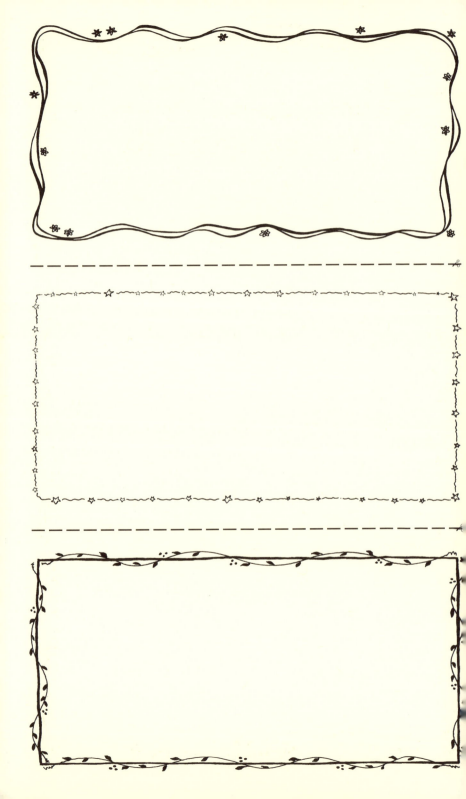

Chocolate-n-Cinnamon Cappuccino Mix

1 1/2 C. sugar
1 C. powdered sugar
2/3 C. instant coffee granules
2/3 C. powdered coffee
  creamer
1/2 C. unsweetened cocoa
1 T. plus 1 tsp. ground
  cinnamon

In a large bowl, combine the above ingredients and stir until the mixture is well blended. Place mix in a wide-mouth 1-quart canning jar.

Attach a gift tag with the directions on how to prepare the cappuccino.

Chocolate-n-Cinnamon Cappuccino

1 1/2 T. Chocolate-n-Cinnamon
Cappuccino Mix
8 oz. (1 C.) boiling water
Whipped cream and chocolate
shavings, optional

Place the Chocolate-n-Cinnamon Cappuccino Mix in a mug. Pour boiling water over the mixture. Stir until the mix is completely dissolved. If desired, garnish with whipped cream and chocolate shavings.

Chocolate-n-Cinnamon Cappuccino

1 1/2 T. Chocolate-n-Cinnamon
   Cappuccino Mix
8 oz. (1 C.) boiling water

Whipped cream and chocolate
   shavings, optional

Place the Chocolate-n-Cinnamon Cappuccino Mix in a mug. Pour boiling water over the mixture. Stir until the mix is completely dissolved. If desired, garnish with whipped cream and chocolate shavings.

Chocolate-n-Cinnamon Cappuccino

1 1/2 T. Chocolate-n-Cinnamon
   Cappuccino Mix
8 oz. (1 C.) boiling water

Whipped cream and chocolate
   shavings, optional

Place the Chocolate-n-Cinnamon Cappuccino Mix in a mug. Pour boiling water over the mixture. Stir until the mix is completely dissolved. If desired, garnish with whipped cream and chocolate shavings.

Chocolate-n-Cinnamon Cappuccino

1 1/2 T. Chocolate-n-Cinnamon
   Cappuccino Mix
8 oz. (1 C.) boiling water

Whipped cream and chocolate
   shavings, optional

Place the Chocolate-n-Cinnamon Cappuccino Mix in a mug. Pour boiling water over the mixture. Stir until the mix is completely dissolved. If desired, garnish with whipped cream and chocolate shavings.

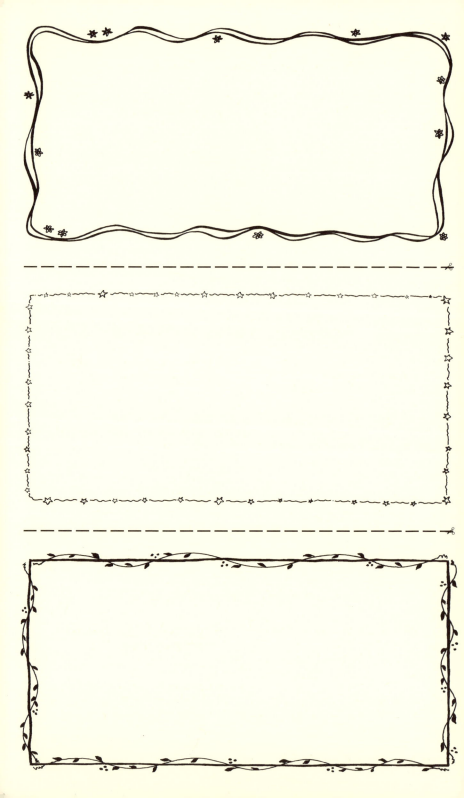

Chocolate-n-Cinnamon Cappuccino

1 1/2 T. Chocolate-n-Cinnamon
Cappuccino Mix
8 oz. (1 C.) boiling water

Whipped cream and chocolate
shavings, optional

Place the Chocolate-n-Cinnamon Cappuccino Mix in a mug. Pour boiling water over the mixture. Stir until the mix is completely dissolved. If desired, garnish with whipped cream and chocolate shavings.

Chocolate-n-Cinnamon Cappuccino

1 1/2 T. Chocolate-n-Cinnamon
Cappuccino Mix
8 oz. (1 C.) boiling water

Whipped cream and chocolate
shavings, optional

Place the Chocolate-n-Cinnamon Cappuccino Mix in a mug. Pour boiling water over the mixture. Stir until the mix is completely dissolved. If desired, garnish with whipped cream and chocolate shavings.

Chocolate-n-Cinnamon Cappuccino

1 1/2 T. Chocolate-n-Cinnamon
Cappuccino Mix
8 oz. (1 C.) boiling water

Whipped cream and chocolate
shavings, optional

Place the Chocolate-n-Cinnamon Cappuccino Mix in a mug. Pour boiling water over the mixture. Stir until the mix is completely dissolved. If desired, garnish with whipped cream and chocolate shavings.

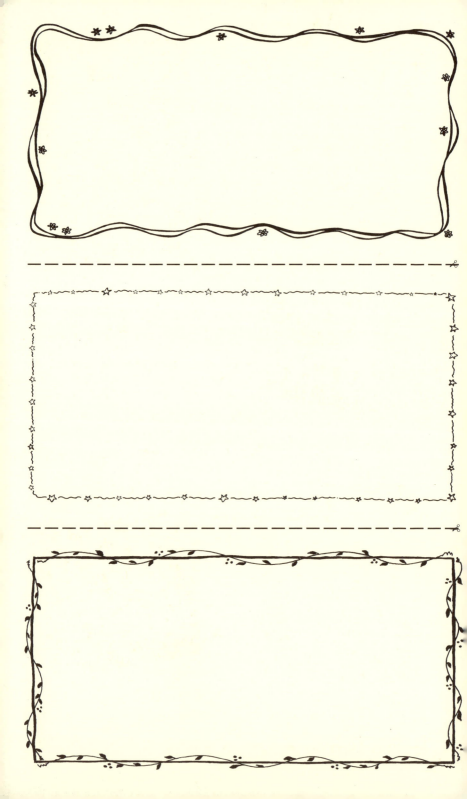